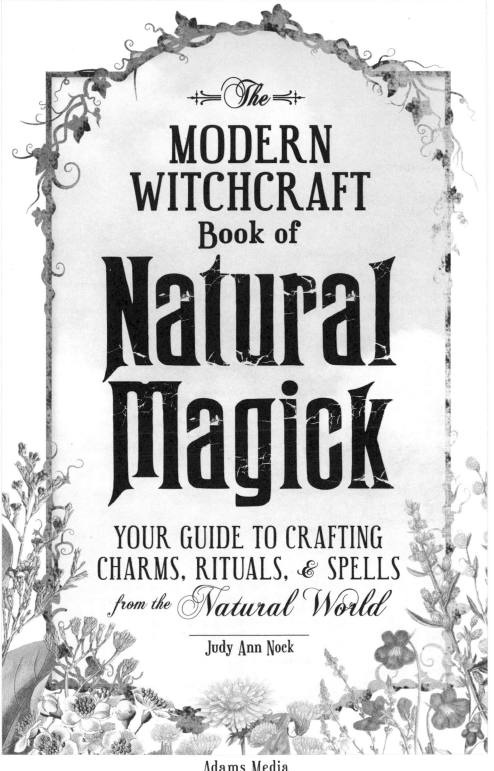

The
MODERN WITCHCRAFT
Book of
Natural Magick

YOUR GUIDE TO CRAFTING
CHARMS, RITUALS, & SPELLS
from the *Natural World*

Judy Ann Nock

Adams Media
New York London Toronto Sydney New Delhi

Adams Media
An Imprint of Simon & Schuster, LLC
100 Technology Center Drive
Stoughton, MA 02072

First Adams Media hardcover edition June 2018

For information about special discounts for bulk purchases, please contact Simon & Schuster Special Sales at 1-866-506-1949 or business@simonandschuster.com.

The Simon & Schuster Speakers Bureau can bring authors to your live event. For more information or to book an event contact the Simon & Schuster Speakers Bureau at 1-866-248-3049 or visit our website at www.simonspeakers.com.

Interior design by Colleen Cunningham
Interior illustration by Kathy Konkle
Interior images © 123RF; Getty Images

Manufactured in China

10 9

Library of Congress Cataloging-in-Publication Data has been applied for.

ISBN 978-1-5072-0720-8
ISBN 978-1-5072-0721-5 (ebook)

To my daughter, Jaime, as the beautiful maiden arises

Acknowledgments

I would like to acknowledge the many people whose support made this work possible, starting with my agent, June Clark, who worked tirelessly to make certain this project would happen. I would like to thank my editor, Rebecca Tarr Thomas, for her impeccable professionalism and ongoing support and responsiveness, and the team at Simon & Schuster, particularly Bethany Carland-Adams and Peter Archer. For radiant inspiration during the times I felt my well would run dry, I thank Leigh Ann Johnson and Dr. Ann Gaba. To the amazingly talented musicians of Psych-O-Positive, with whom I am honored to play and who constantly support and encourage my fascination with the intersection of rock 'n' roll and the occult: Debby Schwartz, Karyn Kuhl, Andrew Gilchrist, and Louie Zhelesnik, where would I be without you? And to my beloved friends who were always there to listen and encourage me: Melissa Chavez, Barbara McGlamery, Sumru Aricanli, Donna Caron, Donna Distefano Thomas, and Tina, thank you. To Amanda Sullivan, thank you for our own private weekly "authors' guild," which helped fuel my focus. Two important institutions were essential to the realization of the project: The New York Public Library, with its unmatched research collections, and The New York Botanical Garden, where I was able to study with Karine Gordineer, master herbalist and the most warm and generous teacher. I would also like to thank my family for their support and for accepting me with all my eccentricities.

CONTENTS

INTRODUCTION

You have picked up this book because something about it appealed to you, something that speaks to your nature, the place where your body and spirit intersect with the environment. Like the excitement in all of nature when a storm gathers, I have that same feeling. Thank you for taking the journey to natural magick with me. We will rediscover our old friends: the grain and corn, the horned and hoofed creatures of the forest, the gentle rain that nourishes and cleanses, the winds that stir, the overwhelming oceans, the bounty of herbs, and the blessed earth mother whom we call Goddess, who will one day cradle our bones. This book is not intended to be another Wicca 101 book; rather, think of it more along the lines of Witchcraft 3.0. Here, you will not find instructions on how to call the directions when casting a circle or explanations of the difference between spells and charms, because I am assuming a level of experience. I write with the intermediate practitioner in mind. I write for the witch who is looking to deepen her connection to natural magick, the priestess who has led many seasonal rituals and is looking for new inspiration. This book is eclectic and inspired by many pantheons. Thank you for choosing this book and for walking the path with me. Do not think you can stay safely inside all the time and still glean from this book. Nature is wild. Run to her. She is waiting for you.

Chapter One

A DREAM IS BORN

The Realm of Seed Magick

Whether we realize it or not, our society is still very much an agrarian one. We are connected to the cycle of the seasons and dependent upon a harvest that many of us share no part in sowing or reaping. Although we may not always intensely feel our connection to the natural world, in practicing magick it is this very connection that we seek to deepen and explore to its fullest. We acknowledge the changing of the seasons as magickal events. We align our intentions with actions in spellcraft that draw heavily on our connection to nature. In the use of herbs, we explore our connection to the Divine Mother: Demeter, Ceres, Gaia, and she who is known by many other names. Whether we seek to honor Abnoba of the Forests and Rivers, Blodeuedd of the Blossoms, or Persephone of the Underworld, the connection to nature is the cord that connects the witch to the Goddess. In many cases, this dedication, this desire to walk a spiritual path connected to the Goddess, begins with a dream. Just as potentiality lies dormant within the seed, so too is the power of magick within us, waiting to be called forth by spells, charms, and rituals. The river of dreamtime flows through our minds like water through the cell walls of a sacred plant. In the tender moments between the worlds, our dreams take form and we are able to name them. These are the seeds of magick, and this is where our journey begins.

Just as the Wiccan year begins with the end, in natural magick our path is rightly attuned to the seed realm. Samhain is summer's end, the time of harvest and of the ancient Greek goddess Hecate. The seed represents the wisdom of the Crone, the elder wise woman who contains all knowledge within herself. The seed is revealed at the end of the life cycle of the plant; it is the product of maturity, perseverance, fertility, strength, and fulfillment. In the perfect unbroken circle, the seed is also emblematic of new life, of possibility, and desire yet to be realized. The equal and opposite powers are balanced within the seed casing, completion and attainment existing concurrently with possibility and opportunity. Seeds are a source of nourishment, both physical and spiritual, and their power is potently creative. In this chapter, we will explore the natural relationships between beginnings and endings through spells and crafts for preparing magickal space; herbal charms to align desire, intention, and action; and meditation and ritual to attune your natural magickal practice to the seed realm.

RITUAL: BUILDING A NATURAL ALTAR

In order to become an adept practitioner of natural magick, you must attune to the earth. This is not something that can be achieved from the comfort of your home. You must go to her. You must explore her wild places. You must immerse yourself in nature and devote some of your gatherings strictly out of doors. To do this effectively, you will need to construct a natural altar.

The altar is a highly magickal and symbolic element in witchcraft. It is the stage upon which a practitioner will interact with the elemental forces of nature and learn of her powerful connections to deity. The altar takes many forms; sometimes it is a mantle over a hearth, sometimes an ornate table. In natural magick, an altar can be constructed from wood or stone, or a combination of both. When used in an outdoor setting, a natural altar becomes a living object. Life is drawn to it, and the practitioner must be able to accept the presence of animals and plant growth, for these are signs that the altar is bound to its environment. Don't clear away the delicate webs of spiders; rather, welcome and work around them. Moss is not scraped away; it is a symbol of the passage of time and the dedication of the practitioner. A natural altar can also be brought into the home and used indoors. Trust your instinct and build the altar that is right for you.

For an altar of wood, consider using a tree stump. Trees are cut down for a variety of reasons and oftentimes you can easily obtain a large and sturdy section. Creating a tree stump altar is also a way to pay homage to the life of the tree that has been cut down. While it is not recommended to cut down a tree for the purpose of creating an altar, in the spirit similar to finding down wood, you may encounter a down tree in the woods, or a tree that has been cut. Inquire if you might avail yourself of a section. If there is a price on the wood, never haggle. This is a taboo when it comes to obtaining magickal tools.

The natural altar is best built outside. You can build a tree stump altar near where you found it. Alternately, you can roll it to another location, or roll it onto a tarp and drag it where you want to place it. Understand your body and your limits. If you need help in claiming your tree stump, arrange for some like-minded souls to assist you in your acquisition. If you are taking from a down tree, sawing off a cross section can be a group endeavor. Rested hands can take over when active hands grow tired. Use heavy gloves and eye protection if you are claiming a section on your own and plan to devote several hours to the task. You can also use several sheets of coarse sandpaper (like 150 grit) to smooth out the surface and remove splinters from the saw cut. It is recommended that the cutting and sanding is done by hand. If the cut is clean enough, you may not even need to sand.

Once you get your tree stump situated, sit beside it and get to know it. Look at the rings and count them. Take notice of the seasons and the years that your altar has weathered. Bring an essential oil such as sage or lavender and use it to trace the rings, starting with the innermost and traveling to the outermost. Take the journey of life with your altar, and look for signs of life within it. There may be insects living within the bark. Accept their presence. You may also smudge the altar as you dedicate it to natural magick.

Another method of creating a living altar is to use three large stones, as large as you can find. You will need a level and a shovel to sink two of them into the ground, standing them upright and as level as you can manage. The third stone is then laid across the other two, forming a dolmen arch. The altar can be anointed, consecrated, and blessed and used for outdoor magick. Dolmen arches were used to mark the gateway to tombs. The dolmen arch altar represents the place where the physical world and the spiritual world separate. The dolmen altar is set at the transition point, and the table stone represents the "stage" where the natural magick practitioner and the elemental spirits, as well as deific energies, may interact.

According to the English poet Robert Graves, ancient Celtic lore holds that the dolmen arch marked the resting place of the goddess Grainne and her consort Diarmuid during their flight of a year and a day. Consequently, this led the dolmen to be connected to the calendar. Graves used the dolmen as a backdrop for the Ogham runes, characters in an ancient Druidic alphabet. Graves set the consonants of Ogham up and across the arch, marking the threshold of the gateway with the vowels. Combined with the threshold, the three stones of the dolmen complete the four-way motif that represents the four seasons, making the dolmen arch a form for an outdoor natural altar. Over time you may observe that the altar takes on and supports life in its own way. Moss may grow and plants may wander across its threshold and up its legs. Welcome these manifestations of life to your living altar. The dolmen represents many things: a gateway, the passage of time, the flight of lovers, the lore of runes, and the changing seasons. Build your dolmen altar and create a connection to the world that births itself anew with each passing year.

RITUAL: PREPARING MAGICKAL SPACE

In creating magick, we are in essence setting the stage upon which the practitioner and the deities may interact. Magickal practice may take place outdoors in a sacred grove or indoors in a ritual space. Our first action, no matter the greater intention, is to prepare a magickal space. This is done by choosing and purifying the space, casting a circle, and calling the quarters. In order to prepare a magickal space suitable for spellcraft, the boundaries must be carefully chosen and clearly defined.

- **Define the magickal space.** This may be an outdoor location such as in the center of a grove of trees. If the land is privately owned, solitary or group work may take place without issue. If you intend to use public land, large groups (typically twenty or more people) will require a permit to gather. Should a permit be in order, contact your local parks department. Usually, a small permit fee is required. This can be shared among group members. If you are solitary, consider enlisting the help of a like-minded friend. The role of a "temple guardian" is an important one. It enables the practitioner to carry out her sacred work in relative safety and peace without the distraction of the possibility of interruption. If you intend to practice magick indoors, the sacred space may be as simple as your altar and its immediate surroundings. You may wish to include an entire room within the confines of magickal space, as the residual energy of a well-crafted spell may give an energetic boost to your surroundings that can last longer than the spell or ritual itself. A simple variation of the ancient practice of "beating the bounds" can be enacted to define sacred space. Walk the perimeter and note your path.

- **Purify the space.** Burning white sage, sweetgrass, or a combination of the two is a popular and effective method of differentiating mundane space from magickal space. The use of white sage has its roots in Native American ritual. It is inexpensive, pleasant smelling, and smolders on its own without the need for charcoal. It differs from garden sage in that it is not used for cooking. Garden sage is closely related to white sage. The leaves are similar in shape but differ in color and texture. Gather white sage into a bundle, called a smudge stick, and briefly light it. Carefully blow out the flame and allow the bundle to smolder. The tendrils of smoke are gently wafted around the sacred space beginning in the east and moving west in a circle. Sage smoke should also be wafted around individuals in a symbolic purification of the physical body that allows the mind and spirit to enter sacred space. Loose white sage leaves can also be lighted either in a ceramic container or on a large shell such as abalone. Use a feather or fan to waft the smoke. If you are sensitive to smoke, as an alternate you can use essential oil of sage to anoint and mark your surroundings. You may place a drop of sage oil on your fingertip, then use it to draw a small circle around an equilateral cross at strategic places to mark the boundary. The oil will make a slight discoloration to certain surfaces, so take this into consideration before you begin.

You may even wish to do a sage oil "test patch" before you use this technique. In an outdoor setting, trees can be marked. Indoors, areas of the floor and walls that correspond to the four directions can be anointed. You may also wish to asperge, or perform a ritual purification, by sprinkling sanctified liquid in the space.

You will need:

- Three teaspoons of pink Himalayan sea salt
- Nine white sage leaves
- A six-inch circle of white cotton fabric
- One yard of red yarn or thread
- A five-sixteenth-inch wooden dowel, approximate length of twelve to eighteen inches
- A chalice of water, preferably from a natural source

Directions:

- In your mortar and pestle, crush the white sage leaves until they are small and coarse. Add the sea salt and mix. Empty the combination of sage and salt onto the center of the fabric. With one hand, stand the dowel on top of the mixture in the center of the fabric. With your other hand, gather together the outer diameter of the fabric tightly around the dowel. Use the yarn to tightly wrap the fabric to the dowel and tie off with several knots. Dip the cloth end of the dowel in your chalice, then use it to sprinkle water around the boundary of your sacred space. Cast a circle and call the directions.
- Preparation is the seed of magickal work. By employing the energy of the elements, you have created a space between the worlds. The fire of the smudging ceremony, the movement of air that allows the smoke to waft or carries the aroma of essential oil, the salt of the earth, and the water from your chalice, attune the space to the natural world no matter where you choose to work your spells. Your sacred space is now ready for magickal purpose.

SEED MEDITATION: CALLING FORTH NEW BEGINNINGS

A seed is a metaphor for the promise of potentiality, the possibilities stored safely within the realm of a magick worker's sphere of influence. We develop a shell to protect our innermost dreams and desires. At times, these longings are so well protected that we cannot access them fully. It is very important to note that the seed will germinate only when conditions are right. In the absence of the correct environment, the seed remains dormant and its potential remains unrealized. In order to summon the potency of seed magick, we focus our energies on creating the ideal environment in which our dreams and desires can flourish. Seed magick shifts our attention inward and demands that we pay close attention to our situation and surroundings. This need can take many forms. It can be our physical environment, home, yard, adjacent land, or our internal landscape, the places of the heart and the thoughts that occupy the mind. The intention of this meditation is to open your mind and spirit to new possibilities through a guided visual journey grounded in nature and focused on envisioning the ideal environment in which your needs will be met.

- Find a comfortable and secure place for meditation, preferably as free from external noise as possible. This can be outdoors or before your altar within the sacred space you have created in the previous exercise. If you are adept at visualization, this meditation will be effective no matter your chosen location; however, doing this work in an outdoor setting is preferred.
- Sit in the lotus position with your spine straight and your legs crossed with your wrists on your knees and your palms facing up. Begin to breathe deeply and rhythmically. Your chest and shoulders should remain still. You are breathing from your core, feeling the breath expand across your back. Close your eyes to focus on your breath. You will begin to take notice of a change in your mental state. As you continue to breathe, allow your mind to clear. Release the mundane world and shift your focus internally on the quiet darkness and the rhythm of your breathing.
- Slowly bring your knees up to your chest. Wrap your arms around your knees and rest your head on your forearms. You should still

be sitting with your spine as straight as possible. Your body is compact and your focus is inward. Your mind is clear. In the calm and darkness, allow your mind to awaken. Visualize the change you seek. Breathe slowly and deeply. Breathe into this dream. You do not need to speak it, only see it in your mind's eye. Visualize the details. Is there a person involved? A new situation or location? Create this new reality according to your deep desire. Give it life by breathing into it. Imagine it in its most minute characteristics. What is the context? Can you identify the sweet perfume of fulfillment? You are the architect of your own desire. Perhaps it is a project completed, or a challenge overcome, or the resolution of a dilemma. Breathe it in and hold the picture of that which you seek clearly in your mind.

- Shift your focus slowly to the external. Feel the air that surrounds you. In your mind, identify the conditions that will aid in bringing your desire to fruition. Visualize your environment according to your will. The seed of your dreams is protected by a shell, kept safe and whole. Now as the ideal conditions are identified, you can begin to let go of your shell. Briefly give energy to the things that stop you, the obstacles in your path, and envision them as permeable, growing thinner, allowing possibility to enter. Protection has its place, but risks must be taken. When safety no longer serves you but rather acts as a barrier to manifestation, it is time to allow change to enter. Breathe into your shell and with every breath allow the hard casing to become flexible. As you continue to breathe, begin to pay attention to the base of your spine. This is the area connected with your root chakra, the energetic organ of the spiritual aura that is most closely associated with survival. For your intention to thrive, it must first survive.

- Breathe into your root chakra and visualize a germinating seed taking root. When conditions are right, the outer casing of the seed shell will become permeable, allowing life to come into being. Just as Demeter is known as "She Who Makes the Seeds Grow," you intone this aspect in your breath. The seed erupts with a delicate tendril of root, searching the supple earth for nourishment. This nourishment is the environment you have envisioned. It is a place of wholeness, of sweetness, of safety and fulfillment. It is your own psychic creation. You breathe into it and give it life. You imagine it in every detail: scope, breadth, and depth. You feel as if this environment has already come into being.

Lore: The Goddess Loses Her Daughter

The goddess Demeter is the source and the sustainer of life on earth. The story of the abduction and restoration of her daughter Persephone is the central classical myth that infuses the change of seasons with divine presence. Persephone is alone when Hades arrives in a chariot from the underworld. The earth splits open, and he emerges with the intention to make Persephone his queen whether or not she agrees. He takes her by force deep into hell. Persephone resists her captor, but when he offers her the fruit of the pomegranate, glistening succulent seeds like rubies, deep red and alluring, she eats a few. When Demeter discovers her daughter is missing, she ravages the earth with winter. A dreadful mourning has seized the heart of the goddess, and her nurturing capacity is replaced by the equally powerful manifestation of her grief. Such is the scope of devastation that Zeus entreats Hades to release his captive queen. Because Persephone has eaten the pomegranate seeds, she is unable to be fully restored to life on earth. For a certain time each year, she must leave her mother and return to the underworld to rule as the queen of the dead. The seed has consigned her to this fate.

Persephone and Demeter are reunited, giving birth to the cycle of seasons. When winter arrives, we are invited to reflect on the quiet and dormant beauty of the earth. Trees are bare of their leaves. Animals hibernate. And the sleeping seed awaits its rebirth with the promise of Persephone's return and the coming spring. When winter arrives in your life, whether it manifests as a fallow period or as a significant loss, remember the promise of the seed. New life will emerge when the conditions are right. Sometimes the best we can achieve is to echo the power of Demeter and endure.

- As you continue to focus your breath on your root chakra, allow your head to turn skyward and relax your knees and arms back into the lotus position. You are ready to receive the light. With the image of sending a network of roots downward, you simultaneously move upward in your mind as well. Breathe deeply with your face turned to the sky and raise your arms into the invoking position: arms extended with palms facing outward to receive the nourishing light. You have the ability to transform this light into energy that will feed your dreams. Continue your cycle of deep breath, slowly shifting your focus from your root to your core, rising steadily to your heart, your throat, your third eye, and finally, the crown of your power. Extend your spine and reach skyward with your arms as far as you can and slowly bring your arms back into the lotus position. Allow the wholeness of your vision to inspire you. Breathe deeply with joy and peace. You are almost there.

- Open your eyes and rest your palms on the ground, allowing time for grounding and centering. Note the changes in your perception. Record any significant insight you have obtained.

SEED RITUAL: THE ELIXIR OF ELEUSIS

The goddess Demeter is one of the most important and powerful among the deities of the classical Greek pantheon. She is often invoked in Wiccan ritual and chants, as she is the embodiment of the Divine Mother. In her relentless search for her daughter, carried off by Hades to the Underworld, she paused and wept in the city of Attica for a period of nine days. The stone upon which she collapsed would become the foundation rock of Eleusis, the location of her most significant temple. For nine days Demeter wept until Celeus and Metanira, the king and queen of Attica, discovered her. Believing her to be a mortal woman gone mad, in compassion they sought to distract her from her grief by placing their two sons, Demophon and Triptolemus, under her care.

During her sojourn in Attica, Demeter was consoled only by the comical and vulgar dance of Baubo and replenished herself with barley water. She would ultimately persuade Zeus to restore her daughter to earth, if only for half the year. The agricultural cycle was established, and for more than 2,000 years, the Eleusinian Mysteries were enacted in Demeter's honor in the fall. The secretive rites were revealed only to initiates. Candidates for initiation would prepare for an entire year, culminating in a nine-day festival called the Greater Mysteries. These celebrations included ritual baths, the pouring of libations, games, sacrifices, and elaborate processions. They rivaled the Olympic Games in their scope and cultural significance.

This ritual libation honors the goddess in her triple aspect and requires advance preparation of several hours or even a day, time permitting.

You will need:

- One cup of pearled barley
- Two quarts of water
- One quarter-cup of honey
- Three lemons for juicing
- A strainer
- A juicer
- A fine grater (for zest)
- A wooden spoon
- A pitcher, carafe, or other container for liquid
- A sprig of mint

Directions:

1. The day before you intend to use the elixir, begin by placing the cup of barley in a fine strainer. Wash the grains thoroughly under running water.
2. As you do so, hold the strainer in one hand and with the other, run your fingers through the grains as they are washed. Think of the effort that has brought them to you: the days of sun and rain, the hands that toiled and sacrificed to bring the harvest home, the life cycle of the plant. Think of how you obtained these grains and if your choices are supporting your intentions. What types of agricultural endeavors are you empowering? Do they align with your path? If they do not, how can you take steps to bring your practice closer to the balance of nature in thought, word, and deed? Allow yourself space to explore the impact of your choices.

3. As you run your fingers through the grain, use this chant:

"Blessed grain, blessed grain. All that dies shall live again."

4. Repeat this chant as a mantra as you wash the grains. Set them aside to drain. In a medium saucepan, bring two quarts of cold water to a rolling boil. Use the wooden spoon to slowly add the grain to the pot while repeating:

"Earth my body, water my blood.
Air my breath and fire my spirit."

5. Gently stir the grains in a clockwise motion and turn the heat down to a simmer. Cover the pot and allow the grains to simmer for forty-five minutes. You can leave the lid slightly ajar as you do not want too much steam to escape. During this time, ground and center yourself and envision your purpose for this ritual. Barley water has long been believed to be a health tonic, rich in nutrients and benefitting digestion; however, this ritual is meant to nourish the spirit.

6. As the power of the seeds is released into the water through this physical and chemical change, reflect upon the nature of your ritual and the potential that it can represent: vitality, healing, the strengthening of bonds, or the easing of grief. Think of the grain as representative of the body, the water as the life force, and the fire that cooks the grain as the fire of spirit, the power of free will that emanates from the solar plexus chakra. The steam that evaporates into the air mingles with the molecules of your own breath. You and the ritual are one.

7. Turn off the heat and rinse and dry the wooden spoon. Allow the liquid to cool before straining it into a vessel such as a pitcher or carafe. If the receiving vessel is not heat tempered, it is unadvisable and extremely dangerous to transfer hot liquid into a room temperature container. While you still want the decoction warm enough to dissolve the honey, wait until it is no longer dangerous to handle.

8. Pour off the liquid into your container through a strainer and set the remaining barley aside for later use. One quarter-cup of honey is about the same as three tablespoons. Use the spoon to transfer the honey one drop at a time into the warm liquid as you say:

> *"The sacred Melissae priestesses sweeten*
> *the worship of the goddess with the offering of the bees.*
> *May the goddess look upon my work and bless it with her sweetness.*
> *May it harm none and be of benefit to all beings."*

9. Stir clockwise until all the honey is dissolved. Using the grater, remove a quarter-teaspoon of zest from one of the lemons by scraping off the yellow portion of the rind, taking care not to include the white portion. With your fingers, sprinkle the zest into the honey and barley water as you say:

> *"As sweet is the love, so is the bitterness of tears.*
> *Such is the balance of life. I accept and honor the equal and opposite."*

10. Begin rolling the lemons by hand against a hard surface to release their juices. When the lemons are supple, use a bolline to slice them and remove the seeds. Press the juices into the honeyed barley water and stir. Your elixir is almost ready. Refrigerate it overnight and garnish with fresh sprigs of mint, allowing several hours for the mint to steep before using. Pour some as a libation into the earth to give thanks for blessings received. Drink with the understanding that you are not just nourishing your physical body; this decoction of grain has been ritually prepared to nurture your spirit and to strengthen your connection to divinity. Drink and be refreshed.

SEED SPELL FOR ATTRACTING LOVE AND OVERCOMING OBSTACLES: THE ORDEAL OF PSYCHE

Perhaps one of the greatest love stories of all time is that of Eros and Psyche. Theirs is an epic mythos of attraction, betrayal, desertion, separation, ordeal, and ultimately, immortal union. So great was the beauty of the maiden Psyche that her admirers worshipped her as an earthly incarnation of the goddess Aphrodite. As her cult grew, the temple of the goddess lay fallow and unattended. Aphrodite was displeased with the abandonment of her temples over the veneration of a mortal woman. She withdrew her favor and commanded Psyche's followers to refrain from adoration. They were instructed to abandon her on the edge of a cliff to meet her fate for angering the powerful goddess of love. Aphrodite instructed her son, Eros, to dispatch the maiden in order to restore proper worship of the goddess. When Eros arrived at the edge of the cliff to do his mother's bidding, he was so struck by Psyche's beauty that instead of doing away with her, he hesitated and wounded himself with one of his own arrows and fell deeply in love with her.

Cautious not to reveal his divinity to the mortal with whom he had fallen in love, he transported her to an opulent dwelling and, carefully concealing himself from her, in the darkness of the night he made her his wife under the condition that she accept the riches and comfort he would provide her without ever revealing his identity or visage. Thus, Psyche was bound to Eros, never knowing that he was a god. He showered her with material comforts, and though she never saw him, she remained with him. Loneliness besieged her and Eros allowed her sisters to visit. Jealous as they were of Psyche's wealth and luxury, they convinced her that her unseen husband must be some kind of monster, for they could accept no other explanation for his insistence on anonymity. They convinced Psyche that she was in mortal danger and that the only way to survive would be to kill her husband.

While Eros slept, Psyche crept into his bedchamber armed with a silver dagger and an oil lamp. When she saw the sleeping Eros, the winged god of love in all his somniculous beauty, she startled and spilled some of the wax from the lamp, burning Eros' shoulder. Awakening in pain to Psyche's betrayal, he flew away. Realizing that her fear and doubt had cost her the love of a god, Psyche was desperate to regain Eros's love. She wandered in heartbroken sorrow and came upon the temple of Demeter, strewn with barley and corn. Demeter advised her to surrender to Aphrodite. Psyche complied and in so doing, Aphrodite charged Psyche with seemingly unsurmountable tasks in exchange for her blessing and her aid in reconciling with her son. In addition to requests for the Golden Fleece and a drop of Persephone's beauty, she charged Psyche with separating a mountain of grains overnight. Distraught by the impossibility of her task, Psyche was on the verge of giving up when a coterie of ants came to her aid and assisted in the sorting. Aphrodite was astounded that Psyche had met her challenges and relented. Psyche was made immortal and was joined with Eros forever.

Love and the longing for love is the desire that draws many practitioners to spellcraft for the first time. This spell echoes the ordeal of Psyche. It is meant to be difficult. The intention is to sustain your focus for an extended length of time, to cultivate patience, and to overcome obstacles. Begin on a new moon and culminate on the full moon so that your task is carried out nightly over the course of fourteen days along the path of the waxing moon.

You will need:

- A large, dark bowl such as a scrying bowl
- Six transparent cups
- A wooden charger or plate from your altar
- One cup of wheat
- One cup of barley
- One cup of millet
- One cup of dried peas
- One cup of dried beans
- One cup of lentils

Directions:

1. On the first night of the new moon, place the scrying bowl on your altar surrounded by the six glasses. Use red jar candles to illuminate your work.

2. Pour the grains individually into the bowl. Invoke Aphrodite as you do so. As you pour, think of the obstacles that are keeping you from your heart's desire. Mix the grains thoroughly with your hands as you articulate the challenges ahead. Meditate by candlelight on the course of action you will take and ask for the aid of the goddess.

3. On the second night, take about a half cup of the mixed grains from the bowl and pour them onto the charger. Stir them with your finger as you focus on a clear path. Using your dominant index finger, trace the letters of your heart's desire into the seeds. Light your candles and begin sorting the seeds into the glasses. This may take several hours. Allow for as much time as you need and free yourself from mundane distractions. Each night as the moon waxes, repeat the ritual:

   - Focus on the action you will take.
   - Envision the obstacles removed.
   - Ask for the blessing of the goddess.
   - Name your desire.
   - Sort the seeds.

4. Little by little with effort and patience your task will be accomplished. The ordeal is meant to illuminate and resolve obstacles that encumber your spiritual growth, allowing the fulfillment of desire to take root and grow. When your task is complete, under the full moon, scatter the seeds to feed the birds and the small creatures of the woodlands, or to find fertile soil and grow. Raise a cone of power and release your intention to the will of the divine universe in perfect love and perfect trust.

The Modern Witchcraft Book of Natural Magick

SEED CHARM TO AID MANIFESTATION

Choose a large seed such as a lima bean. On a small strip of paper, write the idea, desire, dream, or project you wish to call into being. Wrap the strip of paper around the seed. Place the seed and paper together on a circle of green cloth. Place a drop of honey on the paper and a drop of honey on the inside of your wrist. Bring your wrist to your lips to taste the honey and establish your magickal connection to your seed. Your seed has been wrapped in your dream and your dream sweetened by your own hand. Recite:

"By my hand, by the sacred land,
I manifest _____ (name your intention)."

This will be the same intention that you have written on the paper. Give this careful consideration and remember the Rede: "An' it harm none, do what thou wilt" and the Threefold Law, "whatever you send out will return to you threefold."

Gather the circle of fabric together and tie with red yarn, cord, or thread. Pass the bundle through water using the chalice from your altar. Keep it on a small dish upon your altar during the new moon. Find comfort in the darkness, the quiet waiting before your intention manifests. During the waxing moon, bury the charm in the earth.

CHARM FOR OFFERING THANKS AND STRENGTHENING BONDS: A SIMPLE CORN DOLLY

Corn dollies are traditional pagan symbols of the harvest, made from the husks of corn or from sheaves of wheat. The husks and stalks are carefully plaited to form intricate and decorative objects representing gratitude for a bountiful harvest. Corn is a significant crop, and its uses include human food source in the form of whole grain, ground meal, and extracted sugars; major feed for livestock; and even biofuel in the form of oil. Considering the wide impact of corn, using corn in magick invites the practitioner to again examine the implications of personal choice. Before creating the following charm, think about the manner in which corn can be obtained. Do you have a local green market that you can visit instead of supporting large-scale and destructive agriculture? Every step on the path of magick is an opportunity to align with the earth so that your work may harm none and be of benefit to all.

Traditionally, a corn dolly was made from the last standing ear of corn. It represents the spirit of the grain that is cut down and will be reborn. This custom originated in Europe and continues to this day. Meanwhile, in North America, the indigenous Penobscot have handed down the legend of the First Mother, the Corn Maiden who sacrifices herself so that her children can be fed.

You will need:

- A fresh ear of corn complete in its husk
- Four lengths of embroidery thread, cut to twelve inches each; choose colors that please you
- A friend or partner with whom to work

Bonding

While this charm makes a fine solitary craft, its simplicity makes it ideal for friends working together or parent-and-child pairs. Pleasant and easy, it creates a feeling of goodwill and gratitude not only for the harvest but for the relationship between partners.

Directions:

1. Begin with a fresh ear of corn. Run your fingers over the husk and feel the ridges of perfect rows of kernels beneath. Pass the corn between partners to center each other in a shared experience. Think of the ripe ear of corn as a single entity, the life-giving Mother Goddess.
2. Gently remove the four outermost layers of husk and discard. Cautiously continue removing the supple green husks. Choose six pieces, each about six inches long. Lay them out in two groups

of three. As you reveal the golden kernels beneath the husk, acknowledge them as daughters, the promise of the harvest to come. Mother and daughter are one in the sacred circle.

3. Carefully remove the silk from the corn, separating it into two bundles.

4. Make a cross pattern by laying one of the bundles of silk against a neat stack of three green corn husks.

5. Gently gather the husks together around the silk so that it forms a tight loop that the silk is passing through. Hold it together in your hands while your partner uses one of the threads to tie off the loop of husk securely.

6. Fold the bundle of silk in half, forming an interlocking loop with the husk. Have your partner wrap another thread about half an inch from the fold, right above the loop made by the husk. Tie it tightly and cut off any excess thread. Arrange the silk so that it resembles hair. Repeat steps one through six so that each partner has a corn maiden of her own. Keep the effigy on your altar and observe as it begins to turn from green to gold. Say a prayer to it:

"Grain and corn, grain and corn. All that dies shall be reborn."

Seed magick is a potent form of natural magick. In the seed, we can observe the Triple Goddess: the seed is the Crone containing all wisdom within, arising at the end of the life cycle, the culmination of all seasons and many turns of the wheel. We also see the Divine Mother, the bringer of new life, the establishment of the agricultural cycle and the fruits of fertility. The Maiden also dwells within the realm of seed: she is the emerging Goddess; young, innocent, hopeful, and unburdened by change.

The seed realm is where all beginnings and all endings lie. You can attune to this power to aid in bringing about your own attainment: the fulfillment of desire, projects completed, bonds of family and friendship strengthened, and the spirit nourished.

Seed magick is also potent for bringing about endings: situations or relationships that no longer serve you, letting go of old patterns or possessions to make psychic space for the new, or the gathering of strength in the face of impending changes.

As you explore the realm of seed magic, be mindful in your choices. Think about the actions and reactions that will emanate from your spiritual work. Your environment is paramount when invoking the seed realm of natural magick. Continue to grow as well, and allow the seeds of magick to take root, develop, and blossom.

Chapter Two

MAGICK TAKES ROOT

The Woodland Realm

Turning our attention from the seed realm, natural magick now beckons us to shift our energy from our inner world to our immediate surroundings. Just as the seed will not flourish without the correct conditions, so too is our spiritual development inextricably linked to our environment. We are of the land; all life springs forth from the power of the earth. Our path is of the sacred ground, the ground beneath our feet. When we, as witches, speak of *ground*, we are called to look profoundly into that word. The ground is our point of contact with the deep earth. Grounds are also our beliefs, our calls to action, rationales or reasons for setting a course into motion. When we seek to ground ourselves, we wish to center our energy, to prepare for initiation, to connect intimately with the spirits of earth. Beneath our feet are literally millions of microorganisms, an entire unseen realm that teems with unrivaled biodiversity. Creation gives rise to every life-form that inhabits the land. The tiniest wildflower, the myriad forms of lush vegetation, the majestic strength of the stalwart trees, all these send their roots into the ground and spring forth. We walk upon the ground and are always in the midst of the sheer force of life that it issues forth.

Nature is a powerful healer. A simple ritual of walking in the woods, meditating outside of a building, or taking part in the currently popular trend of "forest bathing" can calm the mind and bring about a state of peace. It takes effort to make and to sustain this connection. We have sealed off so much of the ground under the stifling pavement; we spend inordinate amounts of time indoors. There is scarcely any land left that is not within twenty miles of a paved road, and yet the moment we make a conscious decision to reconnect, the forest primeval is there waiting for us in all her glory and fury. Plants, both healing and poisonous, are underfoot coexisting with the beauty and the power of the land. In the creatures of the forest, we hear the swift and quiet footsteps of Artemis the Huntress. In a bed of wild-flowers, we see the loveliness of Blodeuedd. In the verdant greens of the forest glade, we feel the presence of Abnoba. In the rustling wind through the leaves of trees and the lilting songs of birds, we hear the pipes of Pan, the spirit of wild nature. Every flower petal, every leaf, every tree follows a divine pattern. Trees are some of the longest-living beings on the planet.

The trees have their own connections and communications. They are the silent witnesses to our many lives, the keepers of ancestral knowledge. Trees are an integral part of pagan lore. Their magickal properties are both documented and anecdotal. As we explore the woodland realm, we are called to rely upon our intuition and accept gnosis when we encounter its undeniable presence.

Priestesses of the Forest

In classical Greek mythology, the sun god Apollo desired a nymph named Daphne, the daughter of Gaia, mother of the Titans. Apollo pursued her relentlessly through the forest. She rejected him and fled. As Apollo was about to capture her, Daphne asked Gaia for divine deliverance from Apollo's advances. Gaia responded by turning Daphne into a laurel tree. Daphne became a dryad, living as a spirit of the forest, rather than be taken against her will.

The Dryads, or Hamadryads, were known as wood nymphs, goddesses, and priestesses. Revive the tradition of the dryad priestesses by becoming a steward of the forest. Every time you venture out, it will grieve your heart to see the impure and callous treatment of the land at the hands of humanity. Make a pledge to yourself to leave each woodland you encounter a little better for your having been there.

MEDITATION: CENTERING FOR A DEEPER UNDERSTANDING

- Begin by coming into contact with the earth. Go outside, as far as you can from the sounds of the road. Explore your surroundings, whether it is a backyard, a local or state park, or a national forest. Make a commitment to read thoroughly and memorize as much as you can from the following exercise, so that you may take with you the core purpose of this meditation while remaining unencumbered by objects or devices.

- Take a walk in the woods. Listen to the sound of your impact upon the ground. Leaves crunch and twigs snap beneath your feet. Feel the suppleness of the earth as you mindfully walk. With each step there is a slight give as though the earth accepts your path. Look at the trees and notice the patterns of their bark, their boughs, branches, leaves, and twigs. Take note of the time of year and the time of day. Allow your knowledge to influence your perception. You know the earth as Mother, as Goddess. See the denizens of her body as your kindred spirits. Walk with compassion and peace.

- Look for a tree that calls to you. It might be its size or its form that resonates with you. Walk around it, circling slowly. Reach out and run your hands along its surface. Engage with your senses. Think about the scent of the forest: the musk of soil and leaf. Listen with an open mind. Do you hear the wind moving through the boughs? Perhaps you attune to the restlessness and chatter of squirrels and the territorial songs of birds. Think of the life your chosen tree supports: who will seek shelter beneath it or within it?

- Lean your back against the tree. Allow your weight to transfer to the trunk. Experience gravity as you slowly slide your back down the trunk of the tree, finally coming to a sitting position beneath it. Feel the hard roots beneath you and explore the points of contact between the tree, the earth, and your own body. Close your eyes and breathe deeply from your core, keeping your shoulders and upper body still, allowing the breath to expand across your back. Picture the roots extending into the earth, drawing up water and minerals, transforming them into the oxygen you are breathing. Align your breath with the tree, allowing it to fill your core as you slowly lift your arms overhead and press them into the tree trunk behind you as you exhale. Repeat this pattern of breath as you slowly draw your arms down the trunk of the tree until you are touching your own shoulders. Run your hands down your own body as you did the tree. Continue to breathe deeply. When you have reached a meditative state, close your eyes and begin to visualize.

- You are calm and at peace, sitting comfortably at the base of a tree in a grove. Before you is a sprout, a fresh green shoot forcing its way out of the earth and erupting to receive the light of the sun. It grows rapidly, the tender stem so nourished by its thick primary leaves that the secondary and tertiary leaves appear before you. Rising to meet you, the stem thickens and divides into two stout boughs, which divide again into branches that seem to reach for you as would a new friend seeking an embrace. The pale green leaves erupt in a bourgeoning bouquet. The leaves shift before your eyes, moving into layers, gathering into form. The form appears before you as the face of a man watching you from within the boughs. He is in and of the tree. In your meditative state, you have summoned the Green Man, the God of the Forest and Consort of the Divine Goddess.

- The Green Man has come with an important message for you. You look into his deep emerald eyes among the shifting leaves and soon, flowers begin to appear on every branch. They recede as quickly as they burst forth, giving way to the fullness of fruit. The fruit hangs ripe and large, and you now see that an apple tree has grown before you. The tree is your teacher and seeks to illuminate your surroundings through the gift of its fruit. The Green Man emerges, lithe and strong and green as wick wood. He holds an apple before you and requires you to contemplate it.

- You admire the redness and roundness of the fruit. Using a bolline, the Green Man cuts the fruit in half across the middle. He reveals to you the pentagram within, the perfect order of seeds that form the witch's emblem. He makes another cut, this one lengthwise through the previous two pieces, and now the apple is in four pieces. He gives you three of the four pieces. You eat them. You hear a

The Modern Witchcraft Book of Natural Magick

voice like the rustling of wind through leaves. The Green Man is speaking to you and his voice is inside your head like a whisper.

"These pieces you have consumed represent
the oceans where no human, no hoofed nor horned creature,
no bird of the sky nor any other creature of the land nor air may live."

- He cuts the final piece of apple in half and gives it to you. You eat it. Again, his voice washes over and through you like a stirring breeze.

"You have partaken of the body of the Goddess,
Her soaring mountains of rock,
Her frozen tundra and glacial rivers;
nothing that may sustain you grows there."

- He cuts the final piece of apple into four slivers and hands three to you. You eat them and hear his words.

"Nature is wild and untamed.
These are Her deserts, Her marshlands, Her dry riverbeds.
They exist on their own terms and may bring you neither safety,
sustenance, nor comfort."

- There is one tiny sliver of apple left. You watch as the Green Man gently peels off the skin and places it in your hands. You stare at the delicate thin strip, the only thing that is left of the fruit. This you do not eat.

"You hold in your hand all that is left. This is the fertile land that
sustains all human life on the planet. Powerful and small, delicate and
rich, this bountiful and fine layer that resides over the depths of rock is
truly all that you have. All that nourishes you, your ancestors, and your
beloveds is held in this small and sacred space. Keep it safe."

- In the gathering wind, the Green Man retreats into the tree. You watch as he dematerializes, the rearranging leaves that formed his features again appear as they did before. His body melds with the tree, arms and legs transfiguring back to bough and branch. Even though you no longer see him, you feel the strength of his presence. He is the spirit of the forest and does not dwell in any singular place. He is eternal, in and out of time and space.

Land, Earth, and Ground

This meditation was inspired by the work of renowned Italian soil scientist Ciro Gardi. In addition to considering how much is expected and demanded of such a small percentage of the earth, that the relatively tiny amount of cultivatable, fertile ground sustains and nourishes all human activity, domestic animals, and livestock, consider also that the earth upon which we stride is teeming with life; one teaspoon of earth can hold millions of species of microorganisms. There is living energy pulsating beneath our feet with every step on the path. We are now at a point where there is no new land to discover on our planet; only 17 percent of the surface of the earth is truly wild, without any human impact. The long history of the Goddess is hidden within the ruins of ancient civilizations whose artifacts remain covered by the earth.

- You contemplate the tiny strip of apple peel in your hand. You think of how 70 percent of the earth's surface is covered in water. You picture the mighty oceans, savage mountains, inhospitable deserts, all the beauty and fury that resides in the planet. You think of the small piece he has given you and the full impact washes over you. We ask so much of the earth. We build and plow and pave over and demand. Here in the quiet peace of the green wood, you take a step outside the cycle of planting and reaping, of building and destruction to accept nature on its own terms. You do not take anything from the forest but a deeper understanding of the delicate balance upon which we all depend for our survival.
- Slowly open your eyes and drink in your surroundings. You notice details such as the veins on the leaves with new alacrity. Your perception has increased. Carefully and deliberately, rise to your feet. The earth feels different, as though you have put psychic roots into the ground and the ground has accepted you as part of its vast network. You feel the presence of life with every step. The

sound of crackling leaves underfoot reminds you of the great cycle of life. In the forest, nothing is wasted. Energy is returned to the roots in perfect balance. You accept this balance and integrate it with every breath. It is yours to keep.

RITUAL PROGNOSTICA: CREATING A TREE AUGURY

The sacredness of trees is held by many cultures, most notably the early pagans. Wood has been venerated since ancient times and the power of its natural magick is still very much in use today. On your altar, you may have a wand or charger made of wood. These natural objects, infused with magic, are like keys that allow psychic doorways to open. The ritual tool becomes a link between the practitioner and the power of the natural world, allowing a witch to conduct energy, empower ritual, and even receive oracles and messages through the art of divination. The ritual of creating a personal tree oracle is a wonderful companion to the preceding meditation. You have already ventured out into the green wood, and now you have the blessed work of natural magick to perform.

Witchcraft is a form of paganism that involves the veneration of deity and particularly how deity manifests in nature. There is no prescribed dogma, and outside of the Wiccan Rede and the Threefold Law, witches are expected to be ethical in their dealings, spellcraft, charms, and other magickal work, lest the power of the work rebound on the practitioner. Aligning with the spirits of nature is key. The practice of natural magick demands that you leave your comfort zone and that you make regular commitments to have "out-of-building" experiences. Communication and messages are often received through a practitioner's enhanced perception of the natural world; however, in times of confusion, doubt, or challenge, it is sometimes necessary to consult an oracle. Creating your own oracle gives you a more direct and personal plane of reality from which to query. The conduit of this oracle is the wood that you have gathered and prepared yourself.

The second element of the oracle is influence, centered on virtues held by pagans since antiquity and known as The Nine Noble Virtues of Nordic paganism. These are also in alignment with the Brehon

Laws of Druidry. Modern witchcraft is not dogmatic; however, the Threefold Law commands witches to adhere to a moral code of ethics. The Nine Noble Virtues are pagan in origin, and to use them in the context of an augury is to call unto yourself the attribute in highest need of examination to bring about the best possible outcome to your situation.

Pan: God of Wild Nature

In the Greek pantheon, Pan is among the pastoral gods most closely associated with nature and modern witchcraft. Depicted as half man and half goat, Pan possesses a raw sexual energy that teems with a pulsing life force. Known for the captivating music of his reed pipes, Pan has a parallel mythology to Apollo, another god closely associated with music. Pan desired a nymph and as in the story of Daphne and Apollo, the object of his affection was also a daughter of Gaia who spurned his advances. Pan pursued Syrinx, who fled from him, repulsed by his appearance. As he was about to close in on her, Syrinx called out to Gaia, who saved her by turning her into a clump of reeds. Frustrated and defeated, Pan threw himself into the reeds and sighed deeply. The hollow reeds amplified his voice. Intrigued, he gathered seven of the reeds of different lengths and bound them together, creating his emblematic pan pipe, or syrinx, as it is known in Greece.

This oracle is not a fortune-telling device. It is a tool that will focus energy on an appropriate call to action. The action must be taken by you. In both the Druidic and Nordic lines of paganism, the veneration of trees is intrinsic; hence the importance of using down wood, gathered by hand and taken without injury to any tree.

1. Begin by surveying your surroundings. Notice the trees around you, the texture of their bark and the shape of their leaves. Note the time of year and where the trees are in their cycle of bud, leaf, bareness, or dormancy. Start searching the ground for fallen twigs, each about as thick as your smallest finger. You will need nine, each about the length of your palm to the tip of your little finger. It is important that the sticks are not wick; that is, they are taken from the ground and not cut from a living tree. Down

wood is often already dry and easy to work with. In terms of energy, down twigs will contain the residual energy of the full cycle of life, seasons, and time. It is also important that they do not show any rot. The bark should scrape off easily and reveal a light-colored wood underneath.

2. Gather your down twigs together into a bundle and use small garden clips or shears to trim them to the same length. Take some sandpaper (150 grit should work well) and smooth the cut edges. You can also use the sandpaper to remove any remaining bark. Be careful not to sand too much. You want the sticks to be smooth and free of splinters. It is acceptable for them to retain their intrinsic bumps and knots. When the sticks are smooth and rounded along the body and at the ends, take some red paint and paint one tip of each stick. Allow the paint to dry.

3. You will assign a virtue to each stick, either inscribing it in ink or paint or carving the accompanying number into the wood. As you use the oracle to guide and inform upon your choices, you will mix up the sticks, rolling them in your hands. You will touch, feel deeply, and attune with the values represented therein. Meditate on their true meaning. Roll them back and forth between your palms, creating energy and friction. Feel your palms begin to warm. As the energy rises, stop rolling and transfer one stick to your left hand. Open your right hand and let the rest of the sticks fall where they may. The stick you are holding will be your insight into the virtue most closely aligned to your present need.

4. Look at the sticks on the ground. A stick lying on top of others should be interpreted to be a guide to direct you toward the virtue that will bring you to the next place in your journey. Also note the position of the sticks and how they relate to each other. Your sticks should be inscribed in the following way, with the number signifying the virtue of influence written beginning at the painted end and traveling down the stick. Alternately, you can use a word to represent the influence, and then you record the influences in a small blank book or journal for reference. Another option in lieu of a dedicated book is to use the section of your grimoire to include your own definitions of influence alongside their corresponding numbers.

AUGURY OF THE NINE NOBLE VIRTUES		
Number	*Virtue*	*Divinatory Meaning*
1	Courage	Confrontation of fears. Strength in the face of uncertainty. Fortitude. Gallantry. Resolution. Ability to take action that may go unrecognized.
2	Truth	Faithfulness. Sound judgment. Fidelity. Precision. Authenticity. Ability to discern reality. Perceptive mind. Sincere honesty in the face of difficulty.
3	Honor	Veneration. Respect. Recognition. A dignified person. Repayment of debts. Acceptance of responsibility. Fair dealings. Confidence at the decisive moment.
4	Fidelity	Concentration. Steadfastness. Loyalty. Strengthening of bonds. Endurance. Staying true to a course of action. Keeping confidence. Fulfilling an obligation.
5	Discipline	Self-control. Temperance. Scholarship. Dauntless spirit. Steadiness of mind. Composure. Willpower. Mastery. Stamina. Strong sense of purpose.
6	Hospitality	Receptivity. Comfort. A congenial person. Generosity. Social acumen. Warmth. Intimacy. Friendship. Sharing of resources. Stability.
7	Self-Reliance	Independence. Autonomy. Sufficiency. Inner direction. Conviction. Positive influence. Self-assuredness. Pride in abilities.
8	Industriousness	Perseverance. Zealousness. Tireless pursuit of goals. Heightened energy. Diligence. Enterprise. Success in endeavors. A hardworking person. Sustained focus.
9	Perseverance	Endurance. Tolerance. To follow through on a difficult path. Refusal of compromise. Stay the course. Persistence.

These "witch's sticks" provide a thoughtful means of contemplation and communion with the elements of natural magick. Born in nature, imbued with the entirety of the cycle of life and death, they are transformed by your hand into a ritual tool. Use them whenever you

The Modern Witchcraft Book of Natural Magick

have need for guidance, to check in with yourself, or to give insight to others. Record your experiences and commit the virtues to memory. Roll them up in a cloth or make a special pouch or container to hold them and keep them on your altar when not in use. You may also use the gathering of materials as an opportunity to learn about the indigenous trees of your location and their history, biology, attributes, and applications.

A Word on Invocations and Ritual Spells

Whenever you have need to call upon divine energies to interact in your life, it is paramount that you begin with scholarship. As we seek to integrate the powers of the natural world, remember that all of the deities across time and civilization have their own specific mythos. Every word uttered, every color, each sound must be mindfully chosen. Please note that in the proceeding spell for beauty, the Flower Maiden is invoked, for beauty is one of her core features. Blodeuedd is not invoked for love spells because her story is ultimately one of deception and infidelity. In her innocence, she invited a hunting party into her court while her husband was out and fell in love yet again with Gronw Pebr, the lord of Penllyn. She was a fickle one when it came to love, and her husband changed her into an owl. This transfiguration was a permanent punishment. The unfaithful one who sought the company of another became a solitary creature. Her name then changed from Blodeuedd, meaning "flower," to Blodeuwedd, which means "flower-face," and references the appearance of the face of the owl. Her transfiguration caused other birds to fear her.

Solitude is a powerful place of being. The owl is associated with cunning and wisdom. With diligent study, you will grow in understanding of the subtle energies of invocations and how a single letter can signify an entirely different aspect of the Goddess. There is nothing wrong with being alone, but realize the full scope of the energetic and mythological associations of deities and elements before you give voice to invocations.

RITUAL SPELL FOR BEAUTY: HONORING BLODEUEDD

In the Fourth Branch of the Mabinogion, the Celtic book of myth, we learn of the creation of Blodeuedd. The son of the Goddess Arianrhod, Lleu Llaw Gyffes, sought a bride. For him, the Goddess entreated her brothers Gwydion and Math to create the flower maiden, whose hallmarks were innocence, youth, and beauty. Using wands, Blodeuedd was called into being from the flowers of the oak, the flowers of the broom, and the flowers of the meadowsweet. She was called the most beautiful maiden the world had ever seen. Lleu Llaw Gyffes fell in love with her at first sight.

Begin your magick on the evening before a new moon night.

You will need:

- A central altar
- A mortar and pestle
- An abundance of fresh, fragrant flowers
- A quart of distilled water
- A sterilized glass jar with a lid
- A wand

Directions:

1. The night before your ritual spell, wash the flowers thoroughly, trim the stems on an angle, and allow them to sit overnight with the cut ends covered in water. No matter if the flowers were garden picked, wild gathered, or obtained otherwise, you will still need to wash them thoroughly under running water and allow them a day to dry. You want the rinse water to evaporate; you want the blossoms to dry but not to be dried out. When you trim the stems with your bolline, scissors, or shears, try to do so under running water. The moment the stem is cut, the plant will still try to draw water, and the blossoms will be fresher if a wet cut is made. Your bolline will be the preferred tool, provided that it is very sharp. Scissors can compress the stem, while the cut of a knife tends to be neater and allows more water to feed the blossom and keep it enlivened.

2. On the night of the new moon, bring your flowers to your altar. If you are practicing with a coven, invite your companions to bring bouquets of flowers as well. Be sure to communicate with them the preparations beforehand. Let the altar be set with a wand of wood in the east, a single candle in the south, the distilled water in the western quadrant, and the mortar and pestle in the north. The center should be free of any adornment or object. This will be your work space. Begin with a purification rite for all participants, such as those described in Chapter 1. After ritual purification, choose an appropriate meditation to align everyone's energy. Cast the circle and call the quarters. You are now in ritual space and can state the purpose of your spell:

> *"Born of flowers, thou loveliest of maidens, on this dark night*
> *of new moon, we call upon the Maiden Goddess Blodeuedd.*
> *We gather before you to honor your beauty.*
> *Bless us with your grace, that our work may be*
> *pleasing to all and of benefit to all beings.*
> *May the beauty we cultivate within*
> *radiate outward and be received by the world. So mote it be."*

3. Inspect the flowers to be used. Note their fragrance and shape. Begin choosing blossoms to separate from their stems and make a small circle of flowers in the middle of the altar. You can do this alone, or take turns among your companions, going sunwise (that is, clockwise) around the circle. Alternate flowers of different colors and shapes to make concentric circles. Connect them and cross them with flowers of varying colors and shapes to create a flower mandala. Take a single blossom and place it in the center of the circle. Ask the Goddess to accept your work and find it pleasing. The priestess of the ritual (if performing group work) may take the wand and trace the mandala while speaking the request.

4. Take any remaining flowers and separate them from their stems. Place these into the mortar and pestle and gently crush them to release their essence. You should not pulverize them but macerate

with care. Pass the mortar and pestle around the circle so that all companions may inhale their fragrance.

5. Place the crushed flowers into the sterilized jar and cover them with distilled water. Seal the jar. Offer a chant of praise to the goddess and raise a cone of power, directing the flow of energy into the water that holds the flowers. Ground the energy and center all participants. Release the directions and open the circle.

6. Keep the jar on the altar for the next two weeks. On the full moon, strain off the liquid into small bottles or jars. These can be given to participants in the new moon ritual. Use the flower water to anoint the forehead, eyes, cheeks, and heart for a natural link to a beautiful and magickal rite.

GROUNDING RITUAL

What does it mean to be grounded and centered? Grounding is a word that gets bandied about quite a bit but is rarely given the necessary diligent study and practice that it deserves. Grounding is often treated as a ritualistic afterthought, something witches are conditioned to do, often without a rationale. Practitioners of magick are strongly cautioned against the dangers that can come from neglecting to ground one's energy; however, outside of conscious breathing, there is scant information as to what grounding entails or what is supposed to happen when you ground energy. This grounding ritual seeks to illuminate the energy exchange behind grounding so that practitioners are able to execute this technique with greater ability and achieve better results.

When one speaks of being "spiritually grounded," this refers to a psychic state of awareness wherein the powers invoked in ritual have permeated the core being but are not in control of the practitioner. Conversely, neither is the practitioner in control of these energies. Groundedness is an integrated state of relaxation, but not tiredness, of being awake and enlivened, but not overwhelmed by deific or psychic energy. It is a state of balance where energy is accepted, integrated, and returned to the earth. Frequent and effective grounding can produce a store of energy in the practitioner, never a depleted state. In addition to the standard breathing and visualization, this grounding ritual is meant to be used as a consistent part of a greater rite or any other spiritual action or endeavor.

1. Begin by closing your eyes to eliminate further sensory input. Encourage silence in yourself and in those with whom you are sharing sacred space. If you have just raised a cone of power or performed a spell, the heightened energy will be swirling around you and interacting with you on a molecular level. Focus on the points of contact between you and the earth. What you have sent out will return to you threefold, so you will need at least three or more points of contact with the earth. Your feet and hands as well as your backside will be drawn to the earth. Quiet your mind, focus on your breath, and feel.

2. You are feeling the streaming ends of the energy you have directed, like the glowing tail of ice and light that follows a comet. Breathe this energy in and integrate it. On your inhale, direct the energy internally. We are physical beings on a physical plane, so it is natural that you will achieve this through a physical and psychic state. You may begin to feel a sort of tingling inside as you accept the power of your work. You are internalizing your craft. The first component of grounding is an acceptance of power.

3. As you exhale, you are giving some of this energy back to the earth. You are doing this through the established conduits that you opened at the beginning of your work. Grounding is done before the directions are released and the circle is opened. By grounding within the context of sacred space, you are further aligning yourself with the elemental powers of nature. With each release of breath, you are putting something into the environment that was not there before. You are taking something as well.

4. Think of the energy exchange as a bond. Instead of merely sinking your energy into an ambivalent patch of earth, guide your energy with strong intention along the channels of each direction. Visualize yourself at the center of these lines of power. You remain centered and grounded in the very spot where the watchtowers of the east, south, west, and north intersect. Continue sending your

energy along these lines until they encircle the planet and find their way back to you so that you have constructed a glittering net of safety that connects you to your work and protects you from harm. Take as much time as you need. This will ensure your safe return as you step back through the veil into mundane life from your journeys between the worlds.

CHARM: APOTROPAIOI MALEFICIA

Oak is one of the most significant trees in paganism. Held sacred by many cultures, the oak and its veneration have been identified with Druidic worship practices, among other pagan rites. Oak bark that had been struck by lightning was used as a medicine in antiquity. A bit of oak wood burned on charcoal is effective in warding off negative energy. A powerful apotropaic charm can be made by finding a small, smooth, round stone and painting upon it concentric circles in varying shades of blue with a circle of the darkest blue in the middle. Allow the paint to dry and then place the stone on a small indigo circle of fabric. Add a tiny mirror and cover the objects with crushed oak bark. Tie up the bundle with red thread and keep it on your person as an effective ward against evil.

Cloak yourself in green and venture out of doors. Notice the change in air quality and temperature when you step into the woodland realm. Take in the beauty of the land and everything it supports.

Make a commitment to yourself to spend at least a part of every day in nature, whether it is taking a walk in the park, tending a plant, or nurturing an animal. Think of all the ways we connect to nature through the land. We use "land" as a verb to signify an arrival. We use "ground" as a way to connect. We have the earth, the soil, the dirt, the myriad ways we connect with this sacred bridge to the natural world. We have arrived here with a sacred mission: to become stewards rather than sovereigns of the land. We seek to take care of the woodlands and not wantonly destroy them for resources or temporary gain.

Every plant, every animal, every person is connected to the earth. It is impossible for us to be separated from the earth. The force of gravity keeps us firmly planted. There is nothing within the scope of human creation that can support and sustain life while being separated from the earth. Explore the ground and explore your origin, your divine connection. You have immersed yourself in the greenwood. You have identified the deities that dwell therein. Are you ready to go deeper?

Lore: The Power and Importance of Oak

Medieval lore states that Wynfrith of Crediton destroyed the sacred oak tree that grew at Geismar. Known as the Oak of Jupiter and also associated with the Norse god Thor, this tree had great significance among Germanic pagans and was thus targeted by Christians who sought to replace the Old Ways and supplant the worship of pagan deities. Later canonized as a saint and renamed Boniface, Wynfrith used the wood from the sacred oak to build an oratorium, exemplifying the Christian practice of usurping the sacral nature of hallowed pagan sites and appropriating them as emblems of Christian belief.

Oak groves were the gathering places for Druidic rites, according to the writings of Pliny. Oak is also the symbol of Litha, the Sabbat of midsummer when the day is at its longest and the nights finally begin to lengthen. Because of their size, oaks tend to attract lightning, giving oak an association with the storm king gods of thunder. Oaks are believed to be inhabited by nature spirits: *dryad* means "oak faerie." Contemplate the natural cycle of abundance and dormancy when using oak in natural magick. You will soon discover its potency.

Chapter Three

BODY OF THE GODDESS

The Realm of Deep Earth

B eneath the fertile surface of the earth lies an unstable and shifting realm of intense heat and immense pressure. Elements combine and create minerals of untold beauty and wonder. These elements and minerals conduct energy through the earth and through us as well. By opening the mind to subtle energies, we experience divine consciousness on a deeper level. The gifts of the earth are sacred tools to bring us closer to our source, our origin. Powerful and mysterious, it is no wonder that the earliest of civilizations identified the earth as Mother. The 2,000-plus years of patriarchy does not remotely approach the entirety of communal consciousness and how deity is experienced. Archaeological evidence of goddess worship dates to the Neolithic period, between 30,000 and 40,000 years ago. The patriarchal imbalance under which we are currently operating could prove to be nothing more than a fleeting anomaly when viewed through the lens of time.

To practice earth magick means that we make a commitment to understanding nature beyond that which we may readily behold. We endeavor to embrace the cyclical nature of creation, not only in an agricultural sense, but also in the sense that the earth is made up of many layers, and that we experience only a tiny portion. We hold sacred the denizens of earth, and we try to avoid causing harm in our choices. Natural magick demands a level of environmental awareness; once awakened, we cannot go back to sleep and ignore that which we have learned. There is a geographical grid—sometimes referred to as ley lines—that encompasses the earth and makes connections between places of power. Beneath the surface of the earth are layers of rock containing pockets of crystals of indescribable beauty; their compositions are scientifically proven to conduct energy and heat or insulate against energy and heat. Noble metals and dazzling gems, formed far beneath the reach of our eyes, are forced to the surface through volcanic activity. Our imaginations become entranced and we seek unknowable depths, causing destruction in our wake. Knowing what we know, that the earth is sacred, how can we continue to only reap and extract without respecting and protecting? As we contemplate the deep earth, we delve into regions of our psyche aligned with a mysterious, dangerous, beautiful, and wild world.

MEDITATION: CLIMBING THE MOUNTAIN

Any significant undertaking, if it is in the realm of spiritual development, can be validated by the manifestation of an ordeal. The difficult things that are truly worth winning rarely unfold without incident. When an ordeal manifests, you should interpret this not necessarily as something that exists to dissuade you; rather, it is a sign from the universe that you are on the right path, that the work you are attempting is important, that important things rarely come easily, and that you will experience a breakthrough and growth by working through the obstacles in your path. This meditation is designed to help you visualize a metaphorical ordeal so that you can envision how it feels to overcome a challenge in your life. The purpose is to identify and integrate the feeling of accomplishment so that it becomes familiar and resonates within your consciousness.

- Sit comfortably, either upright in a chair or in the lotus position on the floor. Engage in deep, mindful, conscious breathing. Tap into the cycle of energy released and replenished, replenished and released. Breathe rhythmically from your core; your shoulders should not be moving; rather, you will feel the expansion of breath across your back. Close your eyes and focus on that which you need to accomplish. Silently define your goal in your mind's eye. Picture it in detail. When you have given thought to your highest hope, allow a scene to unfold in your mind.
- The sky is a clear, piercing blue with only an occasional feathery cloud drifting by. The air is moved by an unseen wind, not too strong, but just enough so that you notice it. Before you is the base of a mountain covered in foliage. You observe the many

textures of its surface: smooth faces of rock, stony outcroppings, alluring pathways, intriguing plant life, and the sense that this mountain is inhabited by an array of flora and fauna. Toward the top, the density of the woodlands thins out, and you are able to see the majestic peak. You are moved to climb, for you have the strong sense that all that you seek lies at the top of this mountain. You begin to gather reserves of strength. You are called to this journey, knowing it will be difficult, knowing that only with great effort are great rewards achieved. You take a deep breath. You intend to climb.

- The first thing you notice on your ascent is the path. It is worn and easy to find; others have blazed a trail here before you. Among the fallen leaves, the lichens softly enhancing the surrounding smooth rock, the tangle of roots underfoot is a clear path to your goal. You need only follow it.

- Your initial steps are easy; the slope is gentle and yielding. You pull back the occasional branch to pass with minimal effort. You begin to take note of your surroundings: the crispness of the air, the sounds of birds, the scampering of small mammals. You continue your climb as the path gets steeper. You begin to feel the energy that you are using. You lean into your walk, an opposing force to the gravity that pulls you slightly off-balance. As you ascend, you make frequent adjustments to your stride, leaning in or back as the path takes you along a meandering and rambling route. There is no straight path up this mountain. There are times when you doubt your own direction but know in your heart that if you continually head upwards you will be on the correct path.

- Your breathing deepens and your legs strain, but still you forge ahead. You notice a red-tailed hawk, surveying you from the branches of a linden tree. The telltale burnt orange and brown stripes on her feathers allow you to identify her. You are careful not to make eye contact with this avian huntress because you know that raptors can interpret eye contact as a sign of aggression. You bow your head, approaching the encounter with humility and respect. You are seeking communion, not a challenge, and certainly not a challenge in which you will falter. You continue on. High above you in the trees, you see something. You stop and remain motionless. It is a raccoon, eyeing you. You observe quietly and contemplate all the different life-forms on this planet. You are but one of many, each with equal right to inhabit this world. You marvel at the sufficiency of nature, how she provides for all her denizens so that they may flourish. You realize that you have an impact here too. You choose to treat the mountain as though it is a part of you, and you are a part of it as well; take nothing and leave nothing so there is no disturbance. The beauty is yours to behold and not to diminish. You continue your climb.

- The path is growing narrower and steeper. You marvel at the ability of trees to cling to rocky outcroppings and fulfill their life cycles in such precarious places. You begin to gain a deeper understanding of the strength of roots. You consider the roots in your own life, the things that anchor you, that keep you steady, even in the face of danger. Your breath grows short. You still have far to go. Now, it seems that you need the assistance of these unfaltering trees. You grasp for low-hanging branches and pull yourself forward, each step slow and determined. You find yourself having to look ahead and decide where you will take a step before extending your leg, and you need help to balance. But you are alone on your journey and must remain resourceful and determined.

- You begin to tire, and your balance becomes uneasy. Now you are in the thick of it. You slowly sink to your hands and knees. The path is nearly gone, and you scramble from rock to rock, pausing after each maneuver. You stretch your body and reach forward with your right hand, then bend your left leg and gain a foothold. Extending your leg, you gingerly propel yourself forward, reaching now with the left hand, steadying yourself as you climb like an animal, ever close to the ground, ever closer to your animal nature. Your sense of survival begins to activate as all your energy becomes about the climb, the movement of your body, the unpredictable surface, the roots that threaten to trip you, the rocks that are just a little too smooth, and the air that seems to be growing thin. You feel lightheaded, and still you press on. Suddenly, you reach a plateau.

The Modern Witchcraft Book of Natural Magick

- You pause for rest. Your breath steadies and becomes deep and rhythmic once more. You slowly rise to your feet and take a few cautious steps forward. Beyond you lies a valley, seemingly miles away. You are amazed at how far you have come. Above, you can spy the summit. Exhilarated, you realize that through persistence you now have a perspective that you otherwise might never have experienced. Through sheer determination, you have arrived so close to your destination that you may as well already be there. Even the clouds seem closer. And on the wind, there is music. The sound travels through you, and you realize it is a voice with a message meant only for you. You turn your face to the sky. You see the clouds shifting, pulling together with the accelerating wind. They are beginning to resemble an animal. First you see the wings of the hawk, then the wind shifts, and you believe that you see the silhouette of the raccoon. Slowly, every creature that you have encountered on your journey appears before you in the sky. Finally, the quickly shifting clouds take the form of a woman's face, and you know you are in the presence of the Goddess. You close your eyes and an ethereal voice floats through your mind.

"You have tested yourself in your seeking. What have you gained?"

- The question that forms in your mind seems to come from the sky. It catches you off guard. You set off with a goal in mind, and through pursuing your goal, the journey overtook you. You focused less and less on what you set out to achieve and more and more on the abundant life around you, your connection to all beings, the hard and rocky ground, the yielding supple earth, the creatures of the air and land, the sound of the wind overhead, and the sound of branches snapping underfoot. You thought of the contradictions everywhere, how beauty can be treacherous, a task unattainable, and a journey that reaches a climax but that does not quite end. In your mind, you reply:

"I have learned that the beginning is an ending.
To climb, I had to say goodbye to level ground.

And now that I have gone as far as I can go,
I am not quite where I thought I would be.
And the ending is also a beginning.
When I have reached as far as I am able,
I am still only in the middle, for I must return to my point of origin."

- The wind rustles around you in affirmation. You hear the cry of the hawk overhead. You feel the intensity of your altitude. And floating through your mind like a comforting song again is the voice of the Goddess:

"I am the mountain. Its strength is my strength.
You are the mountain; my strength is your strength.
With each step, you bring yourself closer to me, to your source of origin.
There, you will find me, in all beginnings and in all endings."

- Enlivened by Her divine presence, you feel reserves of strength begin to surge within you. You understand that the real work of magick lies in the doing, the singular steps that add up to a journey. Inspired and refreshed, you slowly begin the long, arduous, solitary climb back down.

The Oreades, Priestesses of the Mountain

The guardians and the protectors of the mountains were the Oreades. You can begin to revive this priesthood the next time you take an elevated hike. As you climb to the highest point, recite the following incantation to align yourself with the natural energy of the mountain and all that it contains:

"I have been an earthworm; I know the place where the root and soil meet.

I have been a root; I know the secrets the soil keeps.

I have been a rock; I know the hardness of stone.

I have been a falcon; I know how to hunt alone.

I have been a ram; I know where the edge of the mountain lies.

I have been a tree; I know when each leaf dies.

I have been a cloud; I know where the air grows thin.

I have been the summit; I know when to end and where to begin."

RITUAL: HONORING THE EARTH MOTHER

The ritual of honoring the mother can be done as part of a Sabbat or as a stand-alone esbat rite. In honoring the earth mother, we seek to align our energies with her tremendous power, pay homage, request aid, and give thanks. Your specific ritual will be informed by your own needs and those of the group with whom you are working. This is meant to be highly structured, but within that structure, there is ample space for creativity and authentic devotion. Required skills include knowledge of aspecting; you will need to possess the necessary knowledge to properly invoke the Goddess in her form as Mother and to make the clear connections of mothering in nature.

It is not a requirement to be a biological mother. Mothering is not limited to bringing forth new life; mothering entails maintaining and nurturing that life. In ancient Babylonian artifacts, the goddess Ishtar is often depicted as offering a breast for nourishing a baby. Ishtar exemplifies the concept that the fate of humanity rests not only with the power of the Goddess to bring life into being; rather, her true power is also in her ability to protect, provide for, and guide that life.

1. First you will dress the altar devoted to natural magick. In the east, place a feather. In the south, a lighted candle. In the west will be your chalice of water, and in the north, place a small cauldron of earth or salt. Approach the altar with a purification rite, call the quarters, and cast the circle. If you are solitary, settle into a meditative state. If you are practicing with a coven, appoint a facilitator to lead the meditation. Leading a meditation is also a wonderful activity for those preparing for initiation. The priestess may be focusing on channeling an oracle or delivering the central invocation, and it is appropriate that the ritual duties are shared among coven members. Neophytes can be charged with some of the introductory rites so that they will gain experience in conducting the subtle energies and will be able to rise to the occasion when more is expected from them. The Goddess may be invoked with the Homeric Universal Mother:

"O Universal Mother
Who doth keep from everlasting thy foundations deep

Eldest of things, Great Earth, we sing of thee
All shapes that have their dwelling in the sea!
All things that fly or on the ground, divine,
Live, move, and there are nourished,
These are thine!
These from thy wealth thou dost sustain.
From thee fair babes are born and roots on every tree
Hang ripe and large.
Revered Divinity!"

2. At this point, an oracle may be channeled by the priestess, either extemporaneously or prepared in advance and recited. In the absence of a personal gnosis, the Charge of the Goddess may be used. Next, use sound or singing and chanting to raise a cone of power. When the intensity has been sufficiently built and is reaching a zenith, the priestess will direct the cone to the Goddess and she will direct it where she will. While this basic ritual structure is suitable for many purposes and can be adapted, coming together as a group or as a solitary figure before your altar to honor the earth mother also needs to be done within context; that is to say, the purpose of the rite must be expressly stated and agreed upon by all participants. Some examples of ritual intent are:

   - Consecration of a witch or making a formal dedication to the Goddess.
   - Raising energy to give thanks for blessings received.
   - Honoring the earth mother for the abundance shown forth in our lives.
   - Raising energy to bring about greater awareness about issues affecting the earth.
   - Protecting the earth from environmental destruction.
   - Binding those who would seek to exploit and destroy the natural environment out of greed.

3. After the cone of power has been set to fly into the universe, it is time to ground the energy. All participants must use this time to

give energy back to the earth. Visualization is a helpful tool. If you are not able to practice outdoors and come into direct contact with the earth, you still have the responsibility to penetrate your surroundings with your energy. Have a coven member familiar with grounding, either the priestess or a neophyte, verbally describe where the energy of the group will go. This may include beneath the floorboards, through the foundation and into the bedrock below. Wherever you practice rituals, take time to familiarize yourself with the intimate details of your surroundings so that you can integrate their particular energies into your work and enhance your experience with natural magick.

4. After grounding, the directions and deities invoked are released. These energies are not at the practitioner's beck and call; rather, releasing the directions is a token of respect. Language such as "Stay if you will, and go if you must" honors the connection between witches and the elemental powers by acknowledging the relationship between them without suggesting that any one individual is in control of them. When the elemental powers of the four directions have been released with respect, the circle may be "opened" in that all participants agree that the sacred circle is dismantled for the time being and practitioners return from between the worlds and back into mundane life. This is an excellent time for feasting and merriment. A chalice may be passed, stories are shared, and experiences of individual members are expressed to the group, particularly if an observable affirmation occurred, an oracle was offered, or a gnosis arose during the course of ritual.

SPELL FOR CASTING AWAY

Patterns exist in nature, and we can find wisdom and take comfort within these patterns; however, sometimes we create patterns for ourselves that are harmful. A pattern holds power because it is repeated. Just as magickal words spoken at an auspicious time hold power, just as a sacred rite enacted year after year holds the power of tradition, patterns become embedded deep within our psyches and can sometimes prove to be barriers to fulfillment. Even when we recognize undesirable patterns, recognition does not equal remediation. Just as it takes time and repetition for a pattern to become ingrained, so too must equal energy be spent on dismantling it. This spell is designed to help focus energy on the dismantling of undesirable patterns. It is for casting away the things that no longer serve you. These can be habits, relationships, or even people.

The Importance of Details

Just as scholarship is paramount before invoking deity, so is careful consideration of every element of spellcraft. Every color, sound, scent, and spoken word will affect the outcome. For the Casting Away spell, the dark cloth of the altar is representative of the absorptive power of the earth. The black stones are important because in the absence of color, we are able to project desire into this void. When you find yourself having to make a change to a spell, first consider making a substitution before making an omission. Every component is carefully chosen for a reason. Before making a substitution, determine why that particular element has been put into place and fulfill the purpose even if you need to use something different than what is called for.

The spell is not a banishing spell; it will not block or reverse harmful patterns. It will aid you in gaining strength to cast off the things you no longer need. You will draw upon the powers of the earth, the stark, ambivalent, powerful earth who holds all things, accepts all things, and changes all things. The power of the earth will become your strength, for there is no burden of one single person that the earth is unable to bear. Just as the earth has absorbed artifacts, civilizations, entire species, and the bones of your ancestors, she will accept without question your burden and, through absorbing, release you from it.

You will need:

- A desire for change
- Four tumbled obsidian or onyx stones ranging in size
- A blue or black altar cloth
- Ritual tool

- Time
- Patience
- Dedication

Directions:

1. Begin on a full-moon night. Cleanse and dress your altar and inspect your ritual tools. Remove dust, rededicate and anoint your tools, and place a new altar cloth of dark blue or black on the surface.
2. Place the stones on your charger or altar at the quadrants with the smallest stone in the east, the next largest in the south, the next largest in the west, and the biggest in the north. Do a smudging or asperge on yourself and your sacred space and tools.
3. Quietly call the quarters and cast the circle. Allow yourself to enter a meditative state. Begin to contemplate the pattern you wish to change. Go back to the beginning and remember how it started and determine how you ended up in a place you do not wish to be. Think of the energy you expended creating things that over time you did not want or outgrew. Accept your changing self with perfect love.
4. Pick up the smallest stone. Hold it in your left hand and place your right hand on top, covering the stone. Feel the smoothness against your palm. Project this place of beginning into this stone. Unwind the details in your mind of the things you repeated, that became a part of you, that you now wish to discard. Often, these things are small, and the smallest stone is representative of going back to the beginning, to the origin of the pattern. Carry this stone around with you as much as possible. Observe how limiting it is to carry it. Continue this for four nights, until the first crescent appears in the sky.
5. On the night of the crescent moon, return to your altar. Pick up the stone from the south quadrant. You are no longer contemplating the beginning; you are contemplating your own actions and the ways in which you contributed to your current situation. Unwind them in your mind. If you were manipulated, shield yourself again

future attacks by envisioning yourself standing within a circle of fire. Hold the stone and feel your part in the pattern. Carry it around with you, together with the first stone for the next four nights, until the waxing gibbous moon appears in the sky.

6. On the night of the waxing moon, pick up the third stone and charge it with all the external expectations demanded of you that are connected to these patterns. Begin to envision your life and the choices and energy that will be available once you are no longer empowering the things that you do not wish to grow. Carry this stone along with the other two as frequently as you can. You will become intensely aware of how limiting they can be.

7. On the night of the full moon, take up the largest stone. This is your source of newfound strength. Your burden has grown, but so has your ability to carry it. You are reaching a place of culmination, a new beginning as well as an ending. Name aloud the ways you will cast away the old patterns and begin to formulate a clearer vision of what this will allow you to accomplish. Carry this stone along with the three others to a safe space where you will finally be rid of them all. When you have arrived at your destination, speak these words aloud:

"I release the beginning. What I did not see clearly then,
I see clearly now. I give thanks for the insight I have gained.

"I release the pattern. I created this by my own action and
through my own inaction, and it is within my power to change.
I give thanks for the transmutation of energy.

"I release the expectation. It is not necessary for me to do what I have
always done, and I no longer need to carry things that do not serve me.
I give thanks for the ability to discern.

"I release the burden. Some things grow so heavy that it takes a certain
vestige of strength to bear them but an even greater strength to cast
them away. I now have that strength, and I give thanks."

8. At every charge, throw the stones beginning with the smallest as far away as you can heave them. If you are near a body of moving water, you may throw them in. You can envision them sinking rapidly, settling softly into the silt of the river bottom, slowly sinking into the sopping and welcoming earth. If you are not near a body of moving water, you can throw the stones one by one into a woodland. Throw them as far away from you as you are able. Listen for the sound as the earth welcomes them. They will sit, and you will be free of them. They will gather composting leaves around them. They will endure the rain and sink ever so softly into the welcoming earth, far from your mind. The earth will accept them unquestioningly. They are no longer yours.

QUELLING SPELL: CAULDRON MAGICK

The cauldron has long been held as a symbol of the goddess. Its uses have ranged from the domestic to the demonic. The iconic imagery of the three witches of Macbeth has been etched into our collective consciousness. Dark, strong, and womblike, the cauldron is now primarily used as a magickal ritual tool, dedicated to burning incense or resins or alternately filled with water and used for scrying. It is the latter of these endeavors that will be used in the Quelling Spell. The earth element in the form of stones is also used. Meant to confront and quell any situation that causes distress, this spell can be done either alone or with a group.

1. You will need to begin preparation at least a day in advance. Ideally, you will have a large cast-iron cauldron. First the cauldron must be thoroughly cleaned of any residue from prior use. If you have a traditional cast-iron cauldron, you can use an abrasive such as steel wool and running water to scrub all surfaces, inside and out. This is best done outside if possible. Once the cauldron is cleaned, you can rededicate and consecrate it. On the night of your spell, you (and/or your companions) will need a stone (or several stones) to represent the chaos that needs to be resolved.

2. In the modern vernacular, when people speak of a cauldron, they are often referring to a charged or challenging situation. Some of these might include:

   • A dispute with a neighbor
   • An issue with a coworker
   • A situation where the practitioner has been wronged
   • A confrontation has taken place and the outcome remains unresolved

3. Gather your companions before the cauldron, call the quarters, and cast the circle. Have each participant fill the cauldron with water from the chalice until it is full almost to the brim. Breathe into your stone, give over the discord to the stone, and release the disruption in your mind into the stone. Drop the stone into the water and watch the effects of the disturbance. Ask that the solution be brought to the surface and wait until the surface of the water becomes still once again. Repeat as many times as necessary. When the cauldron has absorbed all the chaos and transformed the disturbance into stillness, sit and scry. Stare deeply into the dark waters and ask for the solution to rise to the surface.

4. Once you have gained sufficient insight, cut an opening in the circle and take the cauldron out. Pour the water into the earth, stones and all. Be careful not to touch the stones. You will never need them again. Let them fall where they may and remain where they fall. Return with the now empty cauldron to sacred space and seal the cut. Continue to meditate or celebrate as the energy directs you. Release the quarters counterclockwise and open the circle with the awareness that your solution will soon arise, but that it will also require action on your part.

RITUAL TOOL: CREATING A PENDULUM

Experiencing the power of gems, crystals, and minerals is a powerful way to tap into the energies of the deep earth. It can take hundreds of years for a crystal to form. Known to conduct energy, quartz crystals are silicates that form layer by layer in pockets of the earth where the silicate is exposed to heat and pressure. A pendulum is an excellent tool for using earth energy to sense beyond. You will need to obtain some 24-gauge copper wire (from a hardware store), a double-terminated quartz crystal, and a length of thread at least one foot long.

1. Before beginning to craft the pendulum, you will need to decide on its use. Do a crystal clearing by either leaving the crystal in a chalice of water outside for a full lunar cycle, or by burying it in the earth from a full moon to a new moon. The method of clearing will depend on your own sense of self. Are you a "down-to-earth" type of person, or do people refer to you as "dreamy"? This first act of dedicating the crystal is to invest in it some of your own energy so that it will work for you.

2. After your crystal has been cleared and consecrated, it is time to begin working it into a tool. With a pair of wire cutters, cut two pieces of wire, each piece about one foot in length. The crystal should have a slight taper. The wider end will be the top of the pendulum and the narrower end will point downward. Place the crystal in between the two pieces of wire and using a pair of chain-nose pliers, twist the two wires together three times on each side starting from the bottom, or the narrower end, of the crystal. Bend the twisted wire up so that it lies against the surface of the crystal. Take the long ends and join them so that they are on the opposite crystal faces of the original twists. Twist these ends together and repeat the pattern.

3. Copper is an element, and a highly conductive one. Continue making a tiny twisted wire cage for your crystal, alternating twists on opposing faces. When you get to the top, twist all four remaining lengths of wire together to form a single torque. Using a small pair of round-nose pliers, bend the torque into a loop and tuck the end inside the loop. Using the wire cutters, trim off any excess. Next, run a thread or cord through the loop and tie it off so that you can slip the thread over your finger and allow the pendulum to dangle.

4. Practice sitting quietly and achieving a sense of peace. Feel the flow of energy from your hand as it runs down along the thread,

through the copper wires, and into the crystal. Attune this new tool, created by your own hands, to the power of magick, which is transformation. You have combined mineral and element in a specific way for a particular purpose. Infuse your purpose into the tool and dedicate it so that it may be of benefit to all beings and perform the task with which you have charged it. You may now use your pendulum for divination, sensing energy, finding lost items, or any other need that would benefit from the presence of natural magick.

PENDULUM PSYCHOMETRY

Using your pendulum to interpret energetic subtleties is an intriguing and fulfilling aspect of natural magick. How you use your pendulum will depend on what kind of information you need it to reveal. It will take some practice at first. The pendulum must be in a state of tension. The tension is created by the force of gravity pulling it toward the earth. The pendulum must also be in a state of balance, meaning that you will have to cultivate a new dimension of stillness. By now, you should be well versed in achieving a meditative state, and this cultivation of inner peace is a key component to successful pendulum psychometry. The pendulum is a tool that will respond to unseen information. This information may come from the surrounding environment, or it may be a product of your own psychic ability. Whatever the source, as both are equally valid, the first act of creating tension is determined by intent and purpose. A pendulum can be used to study an object, either to locate something that is missing or to divine information that would otherwise remain hidden.

The pendulum will also respond to the minute muscular reactions that occur in the natural magick practitioner who is activating her subconscious mind. It is important to move from the meditative state into a trancelike state so that you open yourself to extrasensory perception. Clearing your mind will allow information to flow through you, and it will be observable in the reactions of the pendulum. Honesty is a key component. Without honesty, all you will see is the manifestation of your own manipulation.

Creating the tension and balance lies in the length of the cord, which is dictated by the type of information you are seeking. Some pendulum cords can be a palm's length. Others will need to be longer, depending on your purpose. For example, if you were to use a pendulum for personal divination, seeking "yes" or "no" answers to personal questions, a palm's-length cord will suffice; however, if you are trying to divine information about something that happened in the past in a specific location—a house for example—you will need a much longer cord. If you want to gather information about the age of a rock formation, again you'd use a longer cord. Cord lengths generally range from ten inches up to forty inches. The larger the object or area, the longer your cord will need to be. If you are unsure, begin with a cord just over eight and three-quarter inches, or twenty-two and a half centimeters long.

Sit or stand quietly in a trancelike or meditative state and balance the pendulum so it hangs straight down. You can then ask it to show you "yes" and "not yes" or "yes" and "no." The pendulum will either gyrate or oscillate. In addition to affirmations, you can also observe and count gyrations to set baseline perception. Questions such as "How many rooms are in this house?" are easy to verify. Count the number of gyrations before the pendulum returns to either an oscillatory or still state. You can also inquire about the age of objects. If you are getting a sense of age, you can ask, "Is the number of which I am thinking the age of this object?" and look for either an affirmative gyration or a redirecting oscillation. You can begin by experimenting with artifacts or household objects, even those belonging to other people. This way, you will be able to gauge the accuracy of your psychometric ability.

Trust your intuition and accept that natural magick allows for direct divination from both the environment and from within. Be honest with yourself. If you deliberately encourage the pendulum to sway in a certain way, then you are not truly seeking and should admit this to yourself before practicing further. It is tempting to manifest the answers we hope to find, but with a clear mind and devoted focus, it is possible to transcend such need for affirmation and trust that the power of the earth works in alignment with the natural magick practitioner for an authentic experience.

Earth energies are all around us. The primordial goddesses are among the eldest to whom worship is attributed. Our earliest understanding of deity came through the Divine Mother, the creatrix who brings forth all life, whose body is the earth. Think about the lessons of Gaia; when her daughters were threatened, she rescued them by transfiguring them into nature spirits. The energies of natural magick can be engaged to protect, to shield, and to heal.

When using energies of the earth to aid in your work, understand that you are not directing or controlling the energy; it is much bigger, much older, and much more powerful than you. Approach earth magick with a sense of wonder, an open mind, and a sense of humility. You will find all the wonders revealed to you, the steps of your ancestors, your connection to the land, the living earth that moves within you, inspiring your craft and refining your practice. Remember that you cannot fully attune with the power of earth while remaining in the comfort of your home. You must go to her; observe her in her present state. She is captive beneath the pavement; she is humming below your footsteps. Deep in her pockets of pressure and fire, she is forming gems and minerals from unseen elements. She will reveal her secrets to you only when you go to her and embrace her on her terms, wild as they are. She is everywhere, in the rocks and trees, in the fallen leaf, in the lowly and magnificent creatures of the land. She is in the very air we breathe.

Chapter Four

SYMBIOSIS BETWEEN WITCHES, HERBS, WIND, AND BREATH

The Realm of Air

With every breath, we create and exchange energy between ourselves and the plant world. We are obligated aerobes; without the atmospheric balance of oxygen provided by the plant world, we could not survive but for a few moments. Air is our most immediate necessity. Although we may deprive our bodies of food for weeks, and water for days, without air, we would perish within minutes.

Our breathing is involuntary; how often do we ponder this miraculous transformation? A breath is taken, invisible and easy. Oxygen enlivens each cell in our body, carried along by the streaming internal courses of our blood. We exhale carbon dioxide, which our neighboring plants convert into oxygen, and so a cycle continues and a bond is formed. We are linked through the air we share, and by exploring this elemental connection, we bond ourselves to the natural world. The direction associated with the air is the East, the realm of the rising sun. This is the first quadrant called in ritual, often with the intention of invoking new beginnings just as the dawn begins the sidereal day. Each of us comes into the world through our mother, but individual, helpless, and alone. Our first interaction with the world is to draw breath. The air connects us to our origin as individuals. It is our birthright, a source of individual power, strength, and survival. The air we share connects us with one another as well. It is unseen but surrounds us. The delicate balance that allows us to thrive is directly connected to the plant world. When we explore the realm of air, we connect with the winds of change, the force of hurricanes, the gentle breezes that carry seeds to fertile soil, and the creatures of the air—insects and the migratory birds of the great flyways. Air magic allows our spirits to soar unfettered. Air is the only element that we are not permitted to experience with our eyes, we see only its effects and never its source. This unseen source is a powerful entity in the scope of natural magick.

Creatures of the air bring their own magickal intensity to spells and rituals. Powerful goddesses are depicted with wings, among them are Isis of Ten Thousand Names, The Winged Nike of Victory, and all the denizens of heaven. Winged creatures such as faeries and angels have a purity about them, and they capture the imagination with their relationship to the air and their ability to take flight. Birds and raptors have an aura of magick about them. We think of power and wisdom when we invoke Athena's owl or Horus in his hawk aspect. Even the cherubic depiction of Eros is often paired with a dove. Whether in the mythical, the magickal, or the botanical, our connection to the realm of air is inborn. The breath of our being, the exchange of energy with the plant world, and the migratory paths of birds all pulse with magick. It is involuntary. It is a core component of our physical being and a gateway to worlds beyond our reach. Let your magick take flight and soar as we explore the realm of air.

GATHERING AND PREPARING HERBS FOR STORAGE

Whether you grow your own herbs in a garden or on a windowsill, whether you buy them fresh at a market or forage on your own, using a natural magick practice to procure, prepare, store, and use herbs will strengthen your connections to them. Remember that at all times you are in a symbiotic relationship with the herbal world. It is the air that connects you, and it is the very deprivation of that air that will allow the herbs to be preserved for later use. Depending on the type of herb, there are varying methods for drying and storing herbs. Here, we will discuss the most relevant techniques for where to gather, when to gather, what to gather, and proper storage and shelf life.

Where to Gather

First you must find a wild place. If you live in a city or town, you cannot gather herbs from public parks. In most municipalities, it is illegal to remove any plant material from a public park. Another important reason to avoid these areas is because they are often treated with pesticides. You will need to find a natural setting in a non-polluted area. While not especially difficult, finding a non-polluted area may not be quite as easy as you think. Some areas to avoid are any place near a drainage ditch or swell. Do not gather herbs growing around or near stagnant or slow-moving water. Avoid gathering near power lines and railroad tracks. These can be tempting places because often they offer clear footpaths. This is because these areas are often treated with herbicides. You will also want to avoid roads because plants have deposits of car exhaust on their leaves. Make certain you are at a minimum distance of at least fifty feet from any road before gathering.

If you do not have access to a wild place, consider buying organic herbs. Even with the most sustainable gathering, taking herbs from wild places can lead to depletion. Many people do not think about plants in these terms, but plants can become endangered just as animals can. Do not take more than you can use within one turn of the wheel.

When to Gather

Depending on which part of the plant you intend to use, gathering should be done at different times. If you need leaves, the best time to gather is before the plant goes to flower. Flowering requires huge amounts of energy; the plant will shift its focus to flowering, and the leaves will become depleted. To understand this, take some time to observe a flowering plant. The leaves beneath the blossom will appear limp and sometimes even show browning or yellowing. Before flowering, most of the energy will be in the leaves. If flowers appear, and you need leaves, you are too late. Wait until next year.

Gather flowers and fruit when they appear, normally in late spring to summer in the temperate zone. For roots and bark, the best time to gather is in autumn. In preparation for the coming winter, the plant will shift its energy downward preparing for energy storage, making the roots and bark most potent at this time. There are a few exceptions to these guidelines. For example, coltsfoot will send up a blossom before the leaves proliferate. Always take an illustrated botanical guide with you. Correct herb identification is paramount, and illustrated guides will show you the scale of the leaves in relation to the stem and flowers. Photographic guides are helpful, but illustrated guides are preferred. Photography is subject to angle and lighting, which can make proportion and scale difficult to determine.

What to Gather

Gather leaves on the stem. There is no need to strip them off. Flowers should stay on the stalk if possible. Herbs with smaller flowers such as chamomile can prove difficult to keep on the stem. They have a tendency to fall off. When gathering bark, do not take the outermost layer; these are dead cells. The bark you need is below this surface. Measure about an arm's length from the end of a bough. Use a vegetable peeler to strip off the outer cambium or tissue; the inner bark is the part you want to collect. Roots must be dug up as they grow beneath the surface.

Storage of Herbs

Now that you have gathered, it is time to store. Gather into bunches herbs with woody stems such as rosemary and thyme; tie them with string or bind with a rubber band and hang them upside down. A good way to ensure that your herbs remain clean is to put the entire bundle inside of a paper bag before hanging. This will keep the dust off of them. Moisture is anathema to drying herbs.

If you have grown your own herbs or gathered from a pollution-free area, it is not necessary to wash them before drying. Water can cause herbs to rot quickly. If at any time you see evidence of rot, you must discard your herbs. There is no such thing as picking off mold. Mold spores are microscopic. If you do wash your herbs prior to drying, spread them out and get the moisture off before hanging them for thorough drying. Small flowers and short-stemmed herbs can be laid on a screen or a tray lined with brown paper and turned every other day to allow moisture to evaporate. Thorough drying is important. Since herbs were the earliest of medicines, it has been suggested that the word "drugs" comes from the Anglo-Saxon "dregen" which means "to dry." Drying flowers on a screen will take about a week if there is no humidity. Herbs in bunches will take about four to six weeks to dry. The smaller the bunches, the faster they will dry and the less susceptible they will be to mold.

Five basic factors will degrade herbs. They are:

1. Moisture
2. Light
3. Heat
4. Air
5. Time

You want your dried herbs to be brittle before storing them. Properly dried herbs will retain their color and scent as well as their chemical properties. Minimize light exposure as much as possible during the drying period. The same goes for heat. Many people think that drying near a sunny window is appropriate for herb drying but nothing is further from the truth. A cupboard or closet or even a spare bedroom that stays dark most of the time is far better suited to the task. Even after your herbs are dry, you will want to protect them from light and heat. Tinted glass jars such as cobalt or amber are popular because they block light and act as a natural preservative; however, a clear glass jar wrapped in dark colored construction paper works just as well and is far less expensive. Exposure to heat will weaken the potency of dried herbs. This makes the kitchen a less than ideal storage place. Since herbs are used in cooking and the kitchen is associated with the hearth, it seems like a natural storage place for herbs but puts them at risk of degradation. If you do not have an alternate storage area and need to use the kitchen, keep the herbs as far from the stove as possible.

Time is another factor to consider. Dried herbs will last for about a year before they become less effective. This is important to remember when gathering. As your natural magick abilities expand, consider growing your own herbs and practicing sustainability. In this way, you honor the connections between yourself and the herbs you will use. If growing your own and foraging is impractical, remember to consider buying organic in order to lessen resource depletion. You will find that wonderful things are at work when you practice magick in harmony with nature.

MEDITATION ON THE ZEPHYR WIND

Nature feeds the soul. Find a peaceful place in nature in which to begin this meditation. It can be done as a singular exercise or within the context of a ritual. Its purpose is to allow the practitioner to develop a relationship of perfect love and perfect trust with the wind deities. It is intended to be used as a meditation only, and by no means should the activities described in the visualization be carried out in any way. To stand in the face of a natural element in perfect love and trust is a form of attunement. It means that you accept the elemental powers as natural beings and you approach them with respect and understanding so that you may integrate their energy into your work and receive the benefit of their presence. This meditation is designed to challenge you and help bring you back to center when you feel as though aspects of your life are overwhelming you or blowing out of proportion or otherwise feel beyond your control. Darkness will be confronted and resolved.

- Sit comfortably with your spine straight, your shoulders back, and your face tilted slightly upward. Breathe from your core and pay attention to the exchange of energy. With each breath, you are growing more and more relaxed, but not tired. You feel enlivened. A scene begins to unfold in your mind.
- You are on a journey by foot. A winding path is before you, narrow and perilous. You take deliberate but cautious steps forward. Around you a wild wind swirls, its unruly and unseen reach billowing your robes and rushing through your hair. You walk slowly into the face of the wind. It greets you sharply, blowing tears from your eyes. You begin to give yourself over to its power. As you walk into the wind, tears streak your face and dry almost instantly. You begin to review your path up to this point. The past weighs heavily upon you. With each gust your heart opens as disappointment and tears begin their tortured escape. The wind opens your mind and you see all the paths not taken, opportunities missed, the words you never spoke, the dreams you never admitted, and the great love that you lost. The wind carries your lost hopes through your very being, and you feel as if your soul will crack at their memory.

- Gathering strength from an unseen source, you walk head-on into the wind. The path becomes steeper, rockier, your steps more and more unsteady. You constantly shift your center of gravity as you struggle to remain upright in the face of your fears and the powers of air.
- Ultimately, you come to a place where you can walk no farther. You stand at the very edge of a precipice, and you howl into the wind. It is the cry of catharsis, the drawing in of breath directly into the void where all of your losses reside. There is no one to answer your cry. The wind swallows your voice. Your small and singular breath is no match against the Aurae. There is no one to hear you. You are deep within the hidden realms of your own soul with only a treacherous landscape, an inner storm, and a gathering wind to accompany you. You take a shaking step forward and peer over the edge.
- The jagged edge of the cliff reveals the power of the wind to shape mountains. Beyond this roughhewn shelf, you see through your tears the tidewater mark as another world below comes into view. You see a forest by the water's edge, what appears to be a protected enclave sheltered by the steep cliff arising from the verge of the sea. The water meets the land, playfully lapping against a rocky shore that retreats into a place you can barely discern. It looks so forgiving, so peaceful, so far removed from your tumultuous surroundings. With a heart full of longing, you lean over for a better view. Suddenly, you lose your balance and begin to fall. Your heart drops into your stomach in a wave of fear. You are powerless against gravity, the face of the drop rushing past you at a terrifying pace. Adrenaline floods your body, crying out for you to fight or flee, but you are powerless to do either. You feel that your soul will be torn from your body in a desperate desire to escape. Now that you have let go of the rock, you plummet into a free fall that can only end one way—or so you think.
- The wind suddenly rushes to meet you, buffeting your fall, pushing you upward. For a moment, you are suspended in midair, arms outstretched, able to move your head and look around in all directions. You can see clear across the ocean to distant isles. You

can see where the water joins that land, where the shore retreats to the woodland's edge, and even where the tree line thins and open lush land awaits you. Your heart is stirred by what you see. Slowly, you begin a soft and gentle descent. You know that your fall was not halted by any desire or power within you. You put yourself at the mercy of the winds of change, and Zephyrus, the God of Wind, the gentlest of the wind deities, came to your aid.

- You begin to relax, all tension and resistance leaving your body as you are buoyed up by a powerful but gentle breeze. Slowly along the edge of the sky you drift dreamily until you are gently placed in a prone position on the soft moist grass of an open meadow that lies within the woodland near the shore. The vibrant grasses tremble with life. Wet with dew, the soft blades caress you, and your tears mingle with the moisture on the tender leaves. You breathe your deepest and the grasses respond, accepting your breath, changing it into oxygen and returning it to you. You whisper a prayer of thanks to Zephyrus, and a wind rushes across the meadow, causing all the blades of grass to dance. Your cries subside and change into laughter, your tears of sorrow replaced by tears of relief and joy. You have taken yourself to the edge, you have fallen. Yet you are safe, protected by divine grace. You roll over onto your back to turn your face to the sun. You share the nourishing rays with your plant companions. You breathe together. You take in energy from the sun together. You are unfettered. You are safe. You are at peace.

RITUAL VELIFICATIO: SUMMONING THE AURAE

As the air is the realm of beginnings, invoking the wind can work as a powerful element of ritual, particularly within the context of initiation. If you are preparing a neophyte for initiation (or are a candidate yourself), you may find that invoking the Aurae in the presence of a velificatio (framing veil) is a meaningful piece of symbolism. The veil is a representation of rebirth, of the veil between the worlds, and the separation between the living and the dead, making this an appropriate ritual for Samhain, Imbolc, Litha, or a new or full moon esbat.

You will need six yards of white cotton gauze or muslin fabric, the lighter the better, which is inexpensive and easy to obtain. A bolt of fabric is usually either forty-five or sixty inches wide and will create a beautiful, billowy effect. You will also need an outdoor ritual space with trees, preferably with low-hanging branches. Raising the velificatio can be a solitary or group endeavor, but due to its complexity, it is recommended for group work by eight or more.

1. Begin by preparing the grove for ritual with a smudging ceremony. Decide from where the velificatio will be raised and designate a place for the ritual altar in front of this spot. It may need to be cleared or a flat stone placed so that participants have a place for the altar dressings: tools, flowers, offerings, a conch shell, white candles, or whatever the specific ritual demands. Have two practitioners unroll the fabric and hold it in the air end-to-end lengthwise. A third companion, priestess, priest, or facilitator can pass the smudging stick underneath so that the smoke can waft through the fabric. Participants then agree that by this act, the fabric is purified and transformed from a mundane object into a ritual tool, and then from a ritual tool into a psychic gateway.

2. To construct the gateway, the fabric should be draped with two or three points of contact with the branch of a low-hanging tree. For the solitary or small coven method, a practitioner can roll the fabric up one-third of the way and use the bundled end as a weight to throw over the branch, letting the fabric naturally unroll by gravity, then gathering it up again and repeating so that two lengths are hanging down with sufficient width between them that participants can pass through. Adjustments can be made by having two participants gather up each length and walk slowly away from each other until the fabric is evened out. A solitary practitioner can make adjustments by tugging and walking away to get a clear view or proportion, then making any further necessary adjustments.

3. A more complex method can be done with a larger group and involves a slight bit of rigging. Gather together the center point of the fabric and tie it loosely with approximately three yards of

string or cord. Make a slipknot on one end of the cord and feed the length of fabric through it until you reach the center point, then tighten the slipknot. Use a stick or a stone and tie it to the end of the cord to form a weight. Repeat this twice; once on either side of the center point, each about a yard away. Carefully throw the weight over the bough of the tree, starting with the center, then each side, and pull to raise the velificatio. The three participants who raise the veil can hold it in place during the rite by keeping the weights in their hands, acting as guardians of the gateway and representatives of the triple aspect. Alternately, if the participants do not want to stand as guardians of the velificatio, the cords can be counterweighted with stones, provided that the cord is long enough to reach the ground.

4. Before the velificatio is constructed, all participants should remain outside the circle. Once the velificatio is raised, all companions will undergo a purification rite such as asperge, anointing, or smudging and pass through the veil sunwise around the circle, bringing with them their ritual tools. Once all participants have entered the sacred space through the veil, the ritual altar can be dressed with tools and offerings, even on the ground within the circle but in between the hanging drapes. The velificatio is emblematic of deity dating back to ancient Rome. Begin the cardinal/elemental invocations and add an additional summoning to each one:

(To the east)
"Eurus of the East Wind, I do summon, stir, and call you forth. Most constant one, bringer of new beginnings, we ask you to bless us with your presence. Bear witness to our rite and lend us your aid. Be here now!"

(To the south)
"Auster of the South Wind, I do summon, stir, and call you forth. Storm king, powerful one, we come before you with respect for your force and might. We ask that you bear witness to our rite and lend us your aid. Be here now!"

(To the west)
"Favonius of the West Wind, I do summon, stir, and call you forth.
Most gentle and tender zephyr wind, we ask for your presence
and your favor. Bestow upon us your gentle nature.
Bear witness to our rite and lend us your aid. Be here now!"

(To the north)
"Aquilo of the North Wind, I do summon, stir, and call you forth.
Breath of winter, yours is the cold that transforms water to ice,
that brings forth the snow of Chione. Bless us with your presence.
Bear witness to our rite and lend us your aid. Be here now!"

(To the center)
"I invoke the Goddess and the God, Eos Aurora
of the dawn and Astraeus of the stars! Yours is the
magic place between the worlds where night and day kiss before passing
by each other in an eternal dance of light and grace.
We call upon the Aurae, your daughters,
the Nymphs of the Wind to imbue our rite with your blessed presence.
We seek to honor you and perform acts of love and beauty that
may be pleasing to all. As it is above, so be it below."

5. At this point, blow the conch shell and watch the velificatio for signs of manifestation of deity. The rite may continue as intended by the practitioners depending on the season and their needs. For an initiatory rite, raise a cone of power and bestow the five-fold blessing on the candidate. For a Samhain ritual, speak names of the dead, tell their stories, and share their photos and mementos. During midsummer, a cauldron fire can be lit so long as great care is taken to keep flames a safe distance from the veil. However you wish to incorporate the wind deities, you will find the velificatio creates a wonderful sense of magic and allows for observation of the spirits of air in a unique and symbolic way.

6. When the ritual is complete, it is important to release the wind deities in the same manner in which they were invoked but in opposite order, traveling counterclockwise around the circle.

Language can be adjusted, but the ceremony and respect in the release should mirror the invocations. Some suggested language includes:

"To the North Wind, Aquilo, cold one,
we bid you retreat to the fair isle of Aeolia from whence you came.
Stay if you will, go if you must.
We give you thanks for your presence, your favor, and your aid.
Hail and farewell."

"To the West Wind, Favonius, gentle one,
we bid you retreat to the fair isle of Aeolia from whence you came.
Stay if you will, go if you must.
We give you thanks for your presence, your favor, and your aid.
Hail and farewell."

"To the South Wind, Auster, stormy one,
we bid you retreat to the fair isle of Aeolia from whence you came.
Stay if you will, go if you must.
We give you thanks for your presence, your favor, and your aid.
Hail and farewell."

"To the East Wind, Eurus, constant one,
we bid you retreat to the fair isle of Aeolia from whence you came.
Stay if you will, go if you must.
We give you thanks for your presence, your favor, and your aid.
Hail and farewell."

"To the center, to Aurora and Astraeus and the wind nymphs, the
Aurae, we bid thee retreat to the far corner of the universe wherein you
dwell. As night gives way to dawn, we honor your sacred dance of time
and balance. Stay if you will, go if you must. We give you thanks for
your presence, your favor, and your aid. Hail and farewell."

7. The circle is open but unbroken. Merry meet, and merry part, and merry meet again.

SPELL: INVOKING THE WINDS OF CHANGE

When you find yourself at a crossroads and you are not certain which path to take, you can invoke the Winds of Change to provide clarity. Wind magick contains very specific characteristics that are dictated by the quadrant from which the wind blows. This spell has a "ritual prognostica" quality to it and is characterized by introspection. Think of the spirits of wind as ethereal beings. They will respond to your call, and you are able to experience them directly although they remain unseen. You will begin at home and meditate on the aspect of your life that you seek to change. Then you will journey into nature. Try to accomplish as much of this on foot as possible. Bring a compass and your wand or make your own wind indicator.

There are several ways to identify the wind. Using your wand, you can tie delicate threads or fibers to the end. Stand tall and point your wand up to the sky, letting the threads dangle. Concentrate on their movement and detect the source of the wind. Another way you can track the wind is to make an indicator from a recycled squeeze bottle, such as a bottle of school glue or a nasal spray bottle. Carefully and thoroughly clean the bottle and allow it to dry completely. Fill the bottle with cornstarch. When you come to your quiet clearing in the grove, you can give the bottle a squeeze, releasing a puff of the powdered cornstarch into the air. Watch it carefully, and you will know which energy you are dealing with.

With every step, get a clear focus on what you intend to change. Ask the wind to be your guide, to reveal to you the influences that lie beyond your sight. Ask for their aid, their power, and their presence. Focus on these things as you walk.

1. Find a clearing in the forest or the center of a grove so that you have some open air that is not moving through a thick brush of foliage. First, establish your orientation using a compass. In order to tell from where the wind is coming, you need to know which way you are facing. Meditate on the energies of the Four Winds.

   • The North Wind is representative of power, a strength that is overwhelming and sometimes frightening. If the North Wind manifests during your spell, this is an indication that a major shift will be taking place and you are advised to make any and all necessary precautions to prepare for what is to come.

- The presence of the East Wind indicates a new beginning. This is a favorable omen, in that the change that is about to occur will not be overwhelming but will be in alignment with your desire.
- The South Wind is indicative of passion and possibly a new romance or other type of significant relationship.
- Wind from the West indicates that a resolution is at hand. No matter the trials or conflicts that led you to the cusp of change, manifestation of the West Wind is a sign that peace is on the horizon. Depending on the circumstances, the West Wind can also signify a death, the peaceful repose that follows the toil. Do not be frightened or overanalyze. Sometimes death is symbolic and not strictly physical. It could signify the death of the unwanted pattern or undesirable state of being.

2. Call upon the wind, and as the wind responds, observe your indicators. The more you work with wind magick, the more adept you will become. Eventually, you will find that you are able to call upon the wind of your choice depending upon your need. This is a powerful indication of alignment with natural magick and should be acknowledged with honor.

AROMATHERAPY CHARM: WORKING WITH ESSENTIAL OILS

Of all our primordial senses—taste, touch, and smell—our perception of scent is the most transformative. No other sense activates memories as compellingly as scent. Scent is among our strongest connections to the past; it is also the most evanescent perception of the senses. Scent can act as a warning, alerting us to danger in the environment. Using essential oils is a powerful form of natural magick in that the process of blending oils allows the practitioner to attune with plant energies and integrate them energetically into mind, body, and spirit. Great care must be taken with essential oils. Here, we will explore proper handling and storage of oils, which essential oils are useful to bring about specific outcomes, and how to blend essential oils to create your own scented charm.

Essential oils are concentrated extracts that are volatile and highly aromatic. They can stimulate the senses, calm the mind, invigorate the body, promote wellness and clarity, and assist with spiritual awakenings. When used properly, there is a huge benefit to be gained from incorporating essential oils into your natural magick practice. Because of the volatile nature of essential oils, they readily absorb into the skin and evaporate into the air. You must do your own due diligence and determine beforehand if there are any conditions such as allergies that would be contraindicated in using essential oils. If you have an allergic reaction to any plant, you will also react to its essence. It is also possible to develop allergies later in life. You will need self-knowledge and you will also rely on your intuition, especially when it comes to choosing and blending oils.

An essential oil blend typically has four main components. The first is the carrier oil. Because essential oils are so powerful, they should be handled rarely, never be applied directly to the skin, and never come into contact with injured and broken skin or open sores or cuts. You will need to wear gloves and always use a carrier oil to dilute the essential oil. Suitable carrier oils include jojoba oil (which is actually a wax), avocado oil, and fractionated coconut oil, which will stay liquid at room temperature. In addition to the carrier oil, the blend will have a top note, a middle note, and a base note. The top note is the aroma that you detect first. It will also fade the fastest, and it is the oil that you will use the least of in your blend. The middle note lasts longer, and the base note lasts up to eight hours. Each note exists as a measure of time in addition to a component of fragrance. Different types of essential oils will fall into one of these three categories, with several moving between middle and top notes.

Each essential oil has a therapeutic property from which you can gain a benefit by choosing wisely, experimenting, and using your intuition. The use of therapeutic grade essential oils is highly recommended because they will not contain any petroleum byprod-ucts or other impurities. Some essential oils, such as rose, are very rare, difficult to find, and very expensive. Others, such as lilac, have proven impossible to create. Remember that cost is not always the sole criterion indicative of quality. Allow yourself to experience essential oils and observe their effects. Avoid scents that give you a headache, and allow yourself to be drawn to and work with the essential oils that please you the most.

Use the table for reference when selecting the essential oils with which you desire to work. This is not a comprehensive list, nor do you need to purchase every essential oil, but it will provide helpful guid-ance when selecting oils for blending.

To create a blend, you will need a small glass for mixing, such as a shot glass, and scent strips or clean white strips of card stock to preview your blend. It is also a good idea to have paper towels on hand. You may find that certain essential oils that please you and have properties from which you will benefit do not always achieve olfac-tory cooperation when combined with each other. Use paper towels to remove the oil from your mixing cup. Do not pour essential oil into the sink. Eventually, the oils will accumulate and lead to plumbing problems. Your basic ratio for combining oils to make a blend is 4:2:1. Use the oils sparingly while you are experimenting, and take notes as you go so that you can recreate a successful blend.

Begin with a base note of about ten drops, then add five drops of a middle note, and two drops of a top note. Gently mix with a scent strip and see how the blend affects you. Keep track of your ingredients as well as their effects on your state of mind and sense of well-being. It is advised that you wear disposable rubber gloves while experimenting so that you do not expose your skin directly to the oils. Some oils can function as middle notes and top notes such as:

- Thyme
- Tea tree
- Lavender
- Gardenia
- Clary sage

ESSENTIAL OILS AND THEIR EFFICACY					
Base Notes		**Middle Notes**		**Top Notes**	
Amber	Earthy and grounding	Catnip	Calming, promotes relaxation, and repels insects	Basil	Antianxiety, promotes sleep, brings on menses
Clove	Antifungal and anti-bacterial, warming and stimulation	Chamomile	Anti-inflammatory, calming, and headache relief	Cinnamon	Antibacte-rial, aids respiration
Frankincense	Spiritual growth, grounding and calming	Jasmine	Sensual and calming	Eucalyptus	Antiviral, expectorant, respiratory support
Myrrh	Antiseptic properties, spicy and warm	Lavender	Healing, relaxant, pro-motes healthy sleep	Grapefruit	Uplifting, positive emotions
Oakmoss	Speeds healing, anti-inflammatory and antiseptic	Lemon Balm	Speeds the healing of wounds	Lemon	Immune sup-port, clarity, and emotion-ally uplifting
Patchouli	Calming and grounding	Pine	Respiratory and sinus support	Lime	Disinfectant and uplifts the spirit
Sandalwood	Warm and sweet	Rose	Opens the heart and heals emo-tional wounds	Peppermint	Aids digestion and reduces stress
Gardenia	Antioxidant, reduces headaches	Tea Tree	Powerful healing, antifungal, stimulating	Sage	Magickal and spiritual properties, clearing and clarifying
Vanilla	Antioxidant, aphrodisiac, uplifting	Violet	Reduces stress and insomnia	Spearmint	Stimulating and aids focus

Once you have settled on an essential blend, you are ready to create the charm.

You will need:

- Approximately fifty drops of an essential oil blend
- A glass or metal container such as a small jar that can hold at least half an ounce
- A block of beeswax (you will need one tablespoon grated)
- A grater
- A double boiler
- One tablespoon of carrier oil

Directions:

1. Begin by creating your own essential oil blend. Think of the attributes that you need, experiment, and create accordingly. Take the block of beeswax, grate a tablespoon, and set aside. Using a double boiler, warm the carrier oil and slowly add the grated beeswax. It is best to do this on a gas stove if possible so that you have more control over the flame. You will need to work over a very low flame, as you only need enough heat to warm the oil and melt the wax. Do not overheat and burn the oil. If you do, it will give off black smoke and will not be suitable to use. Your double boiler and grater will have to be dedicated for magickal purposes; they will not be suitable for other use, so keep this in mind before you begin.

2. As soon as the carrier and wax have liquefied together, turn off the heat and carefully pour the mixture into your container. Immediately add your essential oil blend and stir with a scent strip or craft stick. The wax will cool rapidly, so you only have a short window of time to do this. The mixture will cool within half an hour and will be ready to use. You will have a solid oil blend that can be used for a variety of purposes, including anointing ritual participants, dressing candles, and consecrating ritual tools. Your essential oil charm will keep for months if stored in a cool, dry place and will last even longer with refrigeration. With

every breath, the scent will expand your consciousness and create a stronger link between your practice and the natural world.

The realm of air is magickal to behold. Perhaps as a child, you picked a dandelion and blew its seeds into the air, hoping for a wish to be granted. Perhaps you sought the company of faeries, those elusive creatures of air and light. Perhaps you gaze at the sky above, watching in awe as birds and butterflies, dragonflies and bees take flight. The sacred is all around us. It is in the air we breathe. In the power of the wind, the gale force of storm, the breath of meditation, the power of air is undeniable. Take in this power and allow it to inform your magick. Exchange energy with the plants around you and become conscious of this give and take, this inextricable and mutually beneficial relationship. Think about what you are putting into the air. Once you begin the practice of natural magick, it is impossible to remain unaware of your impact on the natural world. Can you begin to make better choices today that will enable you to become a protector of the air? Can you discard air fresheners and instead use your knowledge of aromatherapy? Is public transportation available in your area so that you do not have to contribute excessive carbon to the atmosphere? Can you plant a tree or two and nurture them? Become a steward of the air and seek to balance your impact so that you do not upset the delicate balance in which all our fates are entwined. The breath of life and the power of air rest within you, stir you.

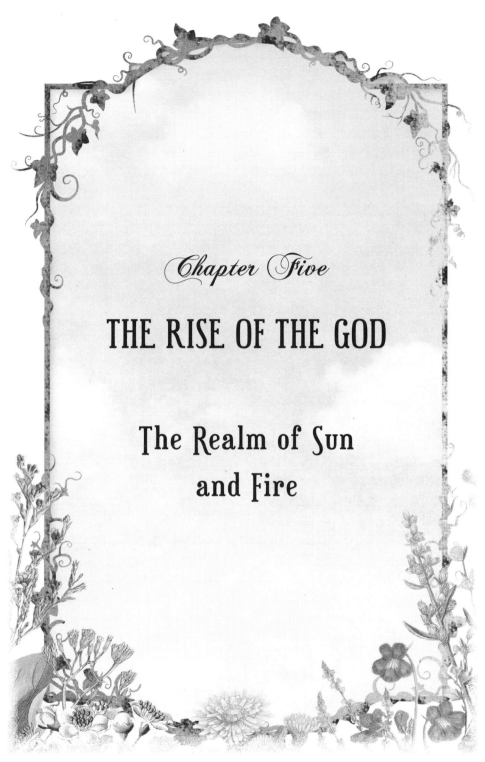

Chapter Five

THE RISE OF THE GOD

The Realm of Sun and Fire

The mighty Helios burns above us in the sky, a constant manifestation of our earliest identification with deity. Solar deities are among the oldest known. The light, heat, warmth, and healing power of the sun was seen both as a god and a gift from the gods. Veneration of the sun, which is essential to all life, dates back to 3000 B.C.E. Archaeological records show the sun frequently depicted as a disc or wheel. The Sun God pierces the darkness with blinding rays; he is called by many names. To the ancient Celts, he was known as Belenos, the Shining One, and by the Welsh name Beli Mawr. His name is the root of Beltane, and his worship was widespread. Depicted with a horse-drawn chariot, a solar disc, and a thunderbolt, Belenos is associated with powerful locations such as the Glastonbury Tor, where even to this day, celebrations of the rising sun are held on Beltane. In Ireland, the Shining One was called Lugh. Consort of the goddess Brighid, Lugh was depicted as a master of many crafts and of war. One of his emblems is the spear.

These solar deities are also healers, generous bestowers of life-giving rays. We require communion with the sun; however, we are also vulnerable in its presence. When the golden rays of the sun fall upon our skin, we are able to synthesize vitamin D in our liver, which allows for calcium absorption into our bones. Vitamin D is found in very few foods, and exposure to the sun is the main way we get it: the vitality of our internal framework is connected to the sun. The plant kingdom is able to transmute the energy of the sun into a source of nourishment. This phenomenon of transformation allows the plants to eat without killing, a feat of which no other life-form is capable. The *via solis* (the path of the sun) dictates our Wheel of the Year; our seasonal celebrations are determined by the position of the earth in relation to the sun.

In classical Greece, there was an undeniable relationship between the sun and Zeus, who was originally perceived as daylight itself. Some of the many descriptive names associated with Zeus are "Zeus of the Burning Face," as he was invoked in Chios, and "Zeus the Scorcher" in Attica at Thorikos. When we invoke the element of fire, we immediately think of passion. Fire defies categorization. It exhibits so many qualities of life; it consumes, leaves waste, reproduces, and requires oxygen. It is so much like life even in how it is created. It is no wonder that ancient cultures assumed that fire was either a gift from or stolen from the gods.

Fire is pure transformation. Anything touched by fire is never the same. Metal is hardened or softened. Water is turned to vapor. Air will feed fire and make it grow. Organic matter can be destroyed, reduced to carbon, purified into its simplest form. Too beautiful to behold with the naked eye, the sun has been associated with powerful gods. In addition to Zeus and Jupiter, his Roman counterpart, solar deities held in high regard include Apollo (Greek), Shamash (Babylonian), and Ra (Egyptian). The sun is our celestial fire and marks the hours of our waking. As Apollo drives his fiery chariot across the sky, so too do we rise to greet the day. The correlation between sun and fire is an essential part of natural magick. Understanding the power and the danger can strengthen your ties to the elements, the earth, and the celestial sphere.

MEDITATION FOR PROTECTION: BEYOND THE GATE OF FIRE

Fire is so powerful that it is feared and should always be handled with great care. Like the serpent, regarded as a symbol of regeneration and wisdom in Wiccan culture but reviled by Christian culture, fire also carries a polarizing charge. While the Christian association with fire is one of damnation, in natural magick, this powerful element is seen as vital to survival. The hearth fire is merry and welcoming. Spells done by candlelight gain an aura of mystery. And the festive bonfires of the Sabbats are unrivaled in their power. Who among us has not felt the rush of excitement when taking a running leap over the Beltane flames? Fire is inextricably linked to natural magick. In this guided meditation, fire is used as an element of protection. Use this meditation whenever you have need of protection, particularly from psychic attacks. Feelings of persecution, being made to feel incompetent or unworthy, belittled or spoken to with sarcasm…these things occur all too often. Having some fire protection is an excellent way to fortify your spirit and protect against wounds of the heart and soul.

- Begin in a comfortable standing position. Close your eyes and begin to draw deep breaths. Increase your rate of breathing so that you are breathing deeply but also very fast. Do not overdo it and force yourself to hyperventilate; rather, your intention is to vary your deep breathing rhythm so that it is somewhat chaotic. The breathing pattern is varied; the depth is not. Bring yourself into a highly oxygenated state with rapid, varying, deep breaths.

- Extend your right hand out directly in front of you. Your index finger is pointed. Point your finger slowly to the ground while continuing the deep and rapid chaotic breathing pattern. From the tip of your finger, focus in your mind on a point on the ground. Focus all your energy into this single point on the ground before you and watch in your mind as a spark erupts. Hold your hand steady and begin to move your right arm, still extended as far as it can go, in an arc. As you trace the arc, a line of fire follows it. The spark continues to ignite. Turn your body ninety degrees to the right, still keeping your arm extended and your index finger pointed. Turn your body slowly and continue the arc, creating a continuous flame. Continue to breathe deeply as you slowly rotate your body, finally ending in the same place where you began, your circle of fire complete.

- Drop your hands to your sides and slow your breathing. Look at the flames surrounding you. They are low to the ground. Inhale deeply and begin to raise your arms over your head. As you exhale, visualize the flames growing higher. The flames are now as high as your reach. You control them with your breath. You breathe into them, and they grow. They follow your command: the flames rise when you raise your arms. You breathe and move, and the flames move with you. You are protected within this circle. Your enemies cannot penetrate it. Whatever they throw at you ignites and gleams red, swiftly turning to grey ash, and fluttering to the ground, never making it remotely close to you.

- You extend your arms to the sides, hands splayed wide open, and the circle of fire reacts. You can send it out as far as need be. You can close your fists and draw your arms in, and the walls of flame respond and draw near to you. You are never harmed by their power—you are kept safe and warm.

- Outside the circle of fire, you can see figures start to materialize. Your guardians of the watchtowers have arrived to lend you their aid. In addition to the circle of fire, you have powerful protectors surrounding you at every quadrant. You have nothing to fear. No harm can come to you. You turn to face them. They return your gaze, beatific and serene. Anyone or anything that wishes to confront you must go through them, and no one dares. Nothing can touch you here. Every slight, each insult turns to ash and disintegrates into the wind. You are fortified and strengthened by the flames. You are able to dance with the fire, joy in your heart, hot blood pulsing through your veins. You are one with the fire, and the fire of spirit lives in you. You have unleashed it in your hour of need and created a gateway between the elements for your own protection.

- Your breathing slows and becomes rhythmical and deep. You lower your arms to your sides, and the flames begin to subside. You extend your left arm in front of you with your index finger pointed. Slowly, you unwind the circle that you had created, but the fire does not extinguish. You draw the spark into your being as you slowly turn to the left. When you have revolved completely, there is a faint line of charred earth around you, but you can still feel the power of fire within you. You sink to your knees and place both hands on the earth, breathing slowly, breathing deeply. Your palms feel very warm, and you bring your hands together as if in prayer, pressing your palms together, compressing the warmth and allowing it to travel across the midlines of your body. You place your right hand over your heart and your left hand over your right hand. You breathe the essence of fire directly into your core. It is yours to keep, yours to conjure whenever you have need. The gate of fire is not to be feared, it is your fiery mantle of protection. You understand it. You respect it. And you are not afraid to use it.

Anima Solaris: Zoomorphism and the Sun

While the worship of solar deities is among the oldest and most widespread of pagan traditions, many animals were venerated as having correlations and connections to the sun. Among these were the eagle, the swan, the horse, the lion, and the stag. The eagle, a superlative hunter and a creature of the sky, was associated with the sun because the eagle's keen eyesight was thought to be able to penetrate anything, much like the rays of the sun. The white swan was emblematic of Helios-Apollo because of the brilliance of its feathers and its noble bearing. The horse was believed to draw the chariots of Apollo and Lugh across the sky. The mane of the lion and the antlers of the stag were thought to resemble the rays of the sun.

RITUAL: THE NINE SACRED WOODS OF THE CAULDRON

Few magickal endeavors are more difficult and more rewarding than starting a fire naturally without the use of accelerants. To the ancient Celts, the Sabbats were known as the Great Fire Festivals. Even in the warmer months, massive bonfires signaled the turn of the Great Wheel. From Beltane fires to the fires of Midsummer, fire has and continues to play a prominent role in ritual and spellcraft. According to the Wiccan Rede, there are nine specific woods for ritual burning. They are:

1. **Birch:** Representative of renewal and beginnings, birch is a self-propagating tree whose twigs and branches are also used as an apotropaic.

2. **Oak:** The oak is symbolic of strength and power; a gateway and one of the most powerful and widely venerated of all trees. The need-fire, the Roman flames of Vesta, and the Litha fires are always of oak.

3. **Rowan:** Representing spirituality and communication, three rowan rods are credited by Celtic lore as the bearers of all knowledge, with scientific wisdom inscribed upon them. The rowan holds and reveals all secrets, except for the name of God.

4. **Willow:** This tree is sacred to the goddesses of the underworld, namely Hecate, Circe, Hera, and Persephone. The willow is also the derivative namesake of the home of the Nine Muses.

5. **Hawthorn:** The harbinger of Beltane, torches of hawthorn were used to ward off bad luck. The scent of hawthorn inspired lust, making hawthorn an antithetical symbol of chastity.

6. **Apple:** The keeper of the pentagram and a symbol of security, the apple tree also represents immortality.

7. **Hazel:** Signifying beauty, wisdom, and learning, the hazel was used in divination such as dowsing and treasure seeking. Hazel was also used in determining guilt and was rumored to give its bearer the power of invisibility.

8. **Grape:** Joy, fertility, magic, and resurrection are the hallmarks of this spiraling vine. Sacred to Dionysus, its strength is thought to be preserved in wine.

9. **Fir:** A female tree, the fir tree is connected with birth, honesty, truth, and resurrection. The cones of the fir tree are used to create the thyrsus, the emblem of Dionysus. The Goddess Cybele transformed Attis (Adonis) into a fir to save him from a mortal wound.

Burning the wood of the elder tree is taboo and should be avoided. This tree is considered sacred to the Goddess and is omitted from ceremonial fires. The white blossoms of the elder tree are symbolic of the White Goddess; to burn this sacred tree is to invite misfortune.

It is not necessary for each wood to be in every ritual fire; rather, you can choose auspicious wood to burn at certain times of the year. For example, an oak fire would be a fitting tribute to the exchange of power between the Oak King and the Holly King at Litha, signifying that the lengthening of days and sunlight's return is upon us. Conversely, the evergreen of the fir can be burned at Yule to remind us that the time of the Green Man is ending and that the long nights of the coming winter are beginning to draw near. Apple would be suitable for a Mabon ritual. Since the blooms of the hawthorn signify the arrival of Beltane, this wood can be included on May Eve. If you are ever in doubt, oak is always a suitable choice. Your magick will grow more potent as you get to know the characteristics and correspondences of the wood you choose. You will create the fire ritual without the use of any lighters or matches. You will pay close attention to the reach of the fire, tend it with care, scry into its flames, and keep it going. Your tasks are numerous, but the result is rewarding.

You will need:

- A safe outdoor space to clear for your fire
- A rake and a shovel or trowel to create a fire pit
- Stones to line the outside of the pit
- A clear glass round lens or magnifying glass
- A few sheets of paper and dry leaves for tinder
- Twigs for kindling
- Logs for fuel, stripped of their bark
- Sand for extinguishing
- A jar candle for keeping the flame
- A pouch for collecting some of the ashes

Directions:

1. Scout your location. If you are planning to use public land, inquire what the local ordinances are. Some types of parks restrict the size and types of fire that you are allowed to build. Find out before you choose your location. Once you and/or your coven have settled on a location, before you begin the preparations, you must first call forth the correct conditions. You will require a bright sunny day without excessive wind. Nothing other than direct sun will suffice. If you have clouds or rain, you will not be successful. Assure

that conditions are right before you begin. This fire ritual can be done either by a solitary practitioner or as a group.

2. Use the rake to clear the area of dead or dry grasses that could provide a fuel source to your fire. Wind can extend the reach of flames beyond what you might intend. Rake away an area greater than you need. Use the shovel or trowel to clear a circle and expose some earth. You do not need to dig deeply; a shallow indentation will do. Fire requires air, so you are creating space for air to circulate below. Use the overturned earth to line the outside of the circle and set it off with stones, either found nearby or brought along by the participants. This will help define the parameters and contain the flames.

3. A ritual fire is built with intention. Each task is undertaken with magickal sensibilities. Be mindful as you gather your materials. Think of their scent, their appearance, their experiences. You are working with all-natural organic matter. Treat it with care and respect. The first task is to gather your tinder. Tinder must be bone-dry. Several handfuls of dried leaves, tiny twigs, dried grasses, moss, or even paper will do. Tinder is the most lightweight of your necessary materials; it will catch fire the easiest and burn the quickest, so you will need lots, probably more than you think. You will make a loose, small pile in the center of the circle of stones. Additionally, you can bring some fatwood to add to the tinder. Fatwood is, as it sounds, twigs or cotton balls soaked in oil such as coconut oil. You can bring a few coconut oil soaked cotton balls with you and pull them apart a bit and add them to the tinder.

4. On each side of the tinder, place a log. Ideally, the logs should be without their bark, as bark will slow the catching. Think about how long you need your fire to burn and factor about one log for each hour. It is recommended that you start with two and add on if necessary. Next, you will need kindling. Kindling wood should also be dry and thin. Wet wood is slower to catch so find lots of dry twigs, no thicker than the width of your finger. You will need these to light from the tinder, so they should be placed above the tinder, balancing across each log like a raft or a ladder. Pile them loosely; remember that air needs to flow in order for the fire to burn.

5. Orient yourself toward the sun. Use your lens to catch and focus a beam of sunlight. The concentrated beam light will begin to smolder anything directly beneath it if it is directed properly. If you roll up a piece of paper into a cone shape, you can start the fire by directing the concentrated sunlight at the tip and blowing ever so gently so that the paper catches fire. If you get a flame, you can use the paper cone to light the jar candle to keep the fire source handy. Alternately, you can add the smoldering paper to the tinder.

6. Blow or fan the embers gently to allow the embers to grow and catch. Add tinder if necessary. Repeat as necessary, adding tinder until the kindling begins to burn. It is important that the flame has room to breathe. Add tinder judiciously; you do not want to smother the flame. Provide circulated air but not too much; you do not want to blow out the flames. You can also light paper, dry leaves, etc. from the jar candle, keeping your concentrated captured sunlight close by.

7. The tinder will burn fast, so keep adding until the kindling ignites. It is a good idea to add reserves of kindling too. Replenish the kindling before the logs catch fire. Once the logs begin to burn, you can add more, laying one or more across the kindling creating a bridge between the original two. The number of logs you add depends on how long you plan to tend the fire. You may need to shift things around to continue providing air flow as the kindling depletes. Move the logs carefully by prodding them with a long stick and allow the embers to catch flame and burn steadily.

8. Gaze into the fire. Observe how the flames shift and transform in shape, bend to the wind, and follow their own pattern of movement. Look for forms and visions. You may see the antlers of a stag appear, or the wild dance of faeries. Take in the scent of burning wood, of turned earth, of the surrounding air. Feel the sting of smoke, the comfort of warmth, the radiant heat. Be present with your fire. Allow it to inspire you, to accept a new reality. Think of it as a source of connection: the four lower chakras are all related to fire. At the base of our spine is the root chakra: fire was essential to survival, providing light and heat and a way to cook food.

Above the root is our sex chakra; passion is often described as fiery. Above the sex chakra is the solar plexus, the seat of our will. A desire to manifest your will in the world is sometimes referred to "fire in the belly." Ascending up the astral body brings you to the heart chakra. A warm heart is considered loving and kind. Even the associative colors of the chakras resonate with the experience of the ritual fire: the green earth of the heart, and the warm orange, yellow, and red of the lower chakras. As you scry into the flames, allow these attunements to amplify your experience, leading you to higher planes of reality. Open your throat chakra. The breath you used to breathe the fire into existence may take the form of a chant:

"Holy Goddess Isis of Ten Thousand Names, fly us on your wings!
Fly us through the flames!"

As you chant, allow the energy to build. Open your mind's eye and see if you can channel an oracle or message from the Goddess. Allow yourself to be open and accept inspiration as it comes to you. Picture the magick and warmth radiating outward into the world so that all beings may benefit.

9. Before the flames die down, take a twig and light it from the ritual fire and use it to light the jar candle if it has gone out. Become the keeper of the ritual flame and protect it or appoint a flame keeper if you are enacting the ritual fire with a group. Take it home with you and use it to light your altar candles. Seven-day jar candles can be lit successively from the ritual flame; see how long you can keep it going. While it is inadvisable to leave unattended candles burning, placing them in the center of the bathtub away from any curtain is something worth considering.

10. Before leaving your ritual space, it is your solemn responsibility as a natural magick practitioner and a steward of the earth to ensure that your fire is properly extinguished. Spread any remaining embers in a shallow layer, and use sand or earth to smother them completely. If you have a water source handy, use water to put out the flames. If you are using earth, sand, or

dirt to cover the embers, make sure that you do not scatter the embers far. Keep them contained within the stone circle. You need to deprive them of air or they will continue to burn, creating a dangerous situation. You must also avoid burying any embers deeply. It is possible that they may continue to smolder, leaving you unaware.

When your ritual fire is completely extinguished and you have your candle, release any deities that you have invoked, give thanks for insights gained, and make mental notes of your experience to record in your grimoire. If you used earth or sand to extinguish the fire, or if you had time to allow it to burn its course naturally and cool, save a few handfuls of the ashes from your sacred fire. You will need them later.

SPELL: NATURAL-DRESSED CANDLE MAGICK

Candle making and candle carving are requisites to magick and incorporate easily into natural magick. While occult shops may offer elaborate and flashy dressed candles covered in glitter, these microplastics have been found to be harmful to the environment. Even though they are created as a spell to bring about an outcome that you desire, the important part of the work is done for you and not by you. It is possible and in some cases even preferable to create a dressed candle with natural ingredients. This candle spell aligns with the lower chakras of survival, sacral, and solar plexus. It is effective in harnessing solar energy in order to accomplish things like creating a feeling of safety and amplifying sensuality and confidence. If there is a situation you need resolved or an imbalance that you need to address, use this spell to aid in the manifestation of your desired outcome.

You will need:

- A specific intention
- A mortar and pestle
- Copal resin, either white or golden

- A red, orange, or yellow jar candle that can be removed from the jar
- Essential oil, coconut oil, olive oil, or almond oil
- Honey
- Bolline or athalme
- Circle template (can be easily made by tracing around a small paper cup on paper and cutting it out)
- A penny

Creating Natural Beeswax Candles

The Melissae were the sacred bee priestesses of Aphrodite. Working with beeswax and honey is a method of attuning with both the natural world as well as the ancient priesthood of the Goddess. Making rolled beeswax candles out of sheets of beeswax is a simple craft that can be enhanced with natural magick. As you did in the dressed candle spell, you can impregnate the beeswax with essential oils and sprinkle resin on the flat sheet before you roll. Use the winding of the sheet wax around the wick as a meditation. You can chant your intention as you roll. These candles are beautiful as altar objects, but since they are already naturally textured, they do not lend themselves as easily to carving.

Directions:

1. Add the copal resin to your mortar and pestle and crush it into a fine white powder. Set aside.
2. Remove the candle from the jar. Using your ritual knife, press the side of the blade across the diameter of the top of the candle, then rotate 90 degrees and press again, creating the pattern of the equal armed solar cross on the top of the candle.
3. Carve three circles equidistant from each other vertically down the candle. You can use a circle template to make the outline. Using your ritual blade, you will scribe a square centered in the lowest circle. In the middle, scribe a smaller circle within the circle, aligned with the top of the outside circle to create a crescent, and in the top one, scribe an equilateral triangle with the apex

pointing downward. The square and the triangle are ancient solar symbols. Combined, they form a pyramid.

4. Take the oil and put three drops into your left palm. Dip your right index finger into the oil in your palm and begin tracing the carvings with the oil starting from the bottom and working your way up. As you massage the oil into the carvings on the candle, begin to formulate the words to your spell in your mind. Speak your desire aloud and incorporate it into a rhyme so that it becomes a chant. You can reinforce your intention with this suggested language:

"By the power of the sun
The magick, unleashed; the spell begun!
Fire, fire, brightly burn
To my will, the fates will turn.
The purpose I do rightly name
Illuminated by candle flame.
By the power of three times three
As I will so mote it be."

Repeat your intention with the chant as you work the oil into all the carvings, including the top.

5. Take a pinch of the powdered copal resin from your mortar and pestle and rub it into the oil. The resin will adhere to the oil and bring out the designs so that they are more visible. The copal is considered a sacred offering, so it has a potency that will transform the candle from an everyday object into an instrument of magick. Make sure that all of the carvings are thoroughly covered.

6. Put a drop of honey on the inside of your wrist. Put another drop of honey at the bottom of the empty jar. As the drop of honey spreads along the bottom of the glass, lick the honey off your wrist and say these words along with your intention:

"May the Melissae, the sacred bee priestesses of the goddess,
bear my intentions aloft. The golden rays of the sun are as honey, pure
and sweet. By my hand, I take part in this bond between the worlds. As
it is above, so be it below. Blessed be."

7. Take the penny and drop it into the jar. As you do so, speak your intention and add:

> *"Element of copper, mined from the deep earth,*
> *be as a channel through which dreams may flow.*
> *This conduit is open to divine energy. May it infuse my work*
> *that it may be of benefit to all beings. So mote it be."*

8. Take the dressed candle and carefully lower it into the jar. If you still have a flame from the ritual fire, you can use it to light your dressed spell candle. Otherwise, use a match. Let the candle burn down and enjoy the results.

HERBAL CHARM: SOLAR CHARM FOR STRENGTH

A charm can be carried with you in your pocket, around your neck, in a medicine pouch, even in your purse. It can be as large or as small as you need it to be. You can make it for yourself or for another person in need. This charm is to aid strength for whatever end you intend to accomplish. That strength may be physical stamina, emotional constancy, or resilience after a challenge. Prepare the charm in the spring or summer months when herbs are available. They can be dried and stored as described in Chapter 4 and saved so that this charm can be made at any time of the year.

You will need:

- A round piece of fabric, natural fiber such as cotton or hemp, linen or silk, and dyed red
- A red cord or yarn to bind the charm
- Equal parts chamomile flowers, dandelion leaves (dried), and High John the Conqueror root
- A bit of gold, either a Sacagawea dollar coin (polished) a small stone painted metallic gold, a fleck of gold leaf, or other representation
- Mortar and pestle

Directions:

1. Create the charm at midday when the sun is at its peak. Combine the three herbs in your mortar and pestle and macerate them together. The chamomile will provide an aura of calm. The leaves of the dandelion are the source from which this important plant gets its name. Let the "tooth of the lion" fortify your strength, your ability to speak out, to protect yourself or your beloveds, to hunt down and capture what you seek. The root of High John will aid in bringing success to your endeavor, and by using a flower, a leaf, and a root, your charm is a balanced herbal being composed of that which draws in and that which sends forth. The gold coin (or other representation) is an emblem of the sun under which you construct your charm. Place all ingredients in the center of the fabric and tie it up tightly. Keep it as long as you have need of it.

2. When you are ready to release the charm, give it back to the earth but do not dismantle it. Keep it whole and give thanks and gratitude. Leave it in your garden or near a favorite tree.

RITUAL AROMATICS: CREATING YOUR OWN INCENSE

Incense has been used for millennia in rites both pagan and ecclesiastical. Use of incense began as a practical necessity when the gods demanded animal sacrifice of their devotees; incense was used to improve the scent of ritual space. Incense was often used to disguise or cover unappealing scents but is more correctly associated with religious practice and sacred rites. Associated with the elements of air and fire, incense itself began to take on a devotional practice of its own as it was seen as pleasing to deities in its own right and not just as an addition to a sacrificial rite. Some traditions make no accommodation for asceticism whether actual or symbolic, where in others it remains a component of ritual. No matter how you choose to practice, using natural elements to create your own incense can enhance your experience with natural magick.

In this section, we will learn about the nature of incense, the main ingredients, and its ceremonial role. Incense in itself can be a powerful ritual if you listen to it. Listening to incense is a practice that requires a refinement of the senses in order to open up new pathways to awareness. Like any other formal ceremony, the incense ritual involves preparation and careful implementation. In the work of Kiyoko Morita, there are enumerated ten virtues of incense, which are attributed to a sixteenth-century Zen priest. They are:

1. Incense brings communication with the transcendent.
2. Incense purifies the mind and the body.
3. Incense removes uncleanliness.
4. Incense keeps one alert.
5. Incense can be a companion in the midst of solitude.
6. Incense brings a moment of peace in the midst of a busy world.
7. When incense is plentiful, one never tires of it.
8. When there is little, still one is satisfied.
9. Age does not diminish incense's efficacy.
10. Used every day, incense does no harm.

The five qualities of taste apply to fragrance and incense as well. These qualities are sweet, sour, hot, salty, and bitter. Sweet scents can be likened to honey or sugar. Sour has the qualities of acidic foods such as plums. Hot is as though a red pepper were held over flames, and salty is the scent of seawater or perspiration. Bitter scents are reminiscent of herbal medicinal decoctions. Familiarizing yourself with these qualities will aid in the success of your experience as you begin to listen to your incense.

The main ingredients of incense include resins, wood, and flowers. Resins used in incense include myrrh, benzoin, and frankincense. Myrrh is a bitter gum plant resin found in Africa and Arabia. Benzoin is a balsamic resin from the *Styrax* genus, a shrubby group of small trees. Benzoin is found in Sumatra, Java, and Thailand. Frankincense is also a gum resin as well as a volatile oil. Like myrrh, frankincense comes from Africa and Arabia. The dried flowers used in incense include star anise, patchouli, and cloves. Star anise is the dried flower of an evergreen found in Vietnam and in China. Patchouli is a shrubby mint from East India that has a distinctly fragrant oil. The dried flower buds of clove spice are found in Indonesia. The woody bark of cinnamon and sandalwood are also traditional incense ingredients. Many of these ingredients can be found at a grocery store or food co-op; for others you may have to visit a specialty store or order.

While there is no shortage of incense ready to buy, creating your own with all-natural ingredients is a fulfilling ritual. Joss sticks, which are slender bamboo sticks coated with incense, are frequently used in ritual not only as an offering but also as a measure of time. A typical five-and-one-half-inch joss stick will burn for approximately twenty-five to thirty minutes and can be used to time a meditation during ritual.

While joss sticks are difficult to make, there are many other ways to prepare incense. To do this ritualistically, you will need several tools, and you will need to gather or procure and prepare your ingredients. It is a good idea to procure ingredients and experiment on your own well before you will attempt the ritual. You may find some incense blends more pleasing than others, and you may also receive a gnosis about what constitutes a pleasing offering to deity. You will need the following ingredients:

- A resin, such as frankincense, myrrh, benzoin, or copal
- A flower, such as clove or star anise, or patchouli
- Bark, such as cinnamon, cedar, sandalwood, or oak
- An egg

Familiarize yourself with the ingredients and think about which ones you would like to combine based on their fragrance and properties. Consider the ratio as well, how much of each you may want to use. Experience them as whole and singular entities before you think about combining them. Then, you will need to gather your tools. You will need mundane tools for preparing the incense as well as ritual tools for the ceremonial use.

You will need:

- A shallow pan, such as a metal baking dish
- A cutting board that fits inside of the shallow pan
- A curved blade with a centered handle
- A mortar and pestle
- A sieve
- An egg
- Two small mixing bowls
- A medicine dropper
- A small wood craft stick
- Paper towel or parchment

Directions:

1. Begin with the bark and put it on the cutting board within the shallow pan. Using the curved knife, aggressively chop the cellulose material into small pieces with rapid, rocking strokes. When the pieces have been broken down, transfer them to your mortar and pestle and combine them with the resin and dried flowers. Continue to crush the ingredients together into smaller and smaller pieces. As the pieces break down, transfer them to the mixing bowl, first passing them through the sieve. Larger pieces left in the sieve can go back into the mortar and pestle for more crushing and grinding so that the process is repeated until you are left with a fine powder.

2. Take the egg and contemplate it. Eggs are a symbol of creation and are frequently depicted in pagan symbolic cosmogony. Crack the egg over the other bowl and observe the golden yolk. After the dark of winter, when food stores were low, the discovery of eggs was life sustaining. The egg became associated with the sun due to the deep yellow of the yolk, and the egg hunt became part of the Ostara Sabbat celebration, born from a survival necessity. Separate the yolk by passing it back and forth between the halves of the shells, letting the clear liquid protein of the white fall into the bowl.

3. Discard the yolk and with the medicine dropper, transfer the egg white into the powdered incense and begin mixing it together with a small wooden craft stick. Use just enough so that the powder comes together. You do not want it too wet. The consistency should be similar to dough. Depending on how much incense powder you are able to make, you will probably not need the entire white. Approximately three teaspoons of incense powder will hold together nicely only using about two-thirds of the white of one egg. The yield from this amount will be around eight individual incense cones. Shape the mixture with your fingers into a small pyramid or cone, each about one-half inch tall. Place them on a paper towel or parchment paper on a sunny windowsill and allow them to dry at least twenty-four hours.

When your incense is dry and ready to use, you will need:

- A small cauldron or ceramic bowl
- Trivet
- Ashes from your last ritual fire
- A small round charcoal
- Bolline
- Fire source

Directions:

1. To begin the ritual, bring your incense and tools to your altar. Place the cauldron or ceramic bowl on the trivet and fill it about two-thirds full with ashes. Light the charcoal and push it into the ash with the bolline. Allow it to turn gray before adding your incense. Place the cone or ball on top of the charcoal and allow the smoke to waft over your clothes and your body.
2. Sit quietly and allow the scent to transport you. See if you can identify the individual components of your blend. Feel the transmutation of aromatic wood, exotic flowers, and resins from the far corners of the earth. Reflect on your process, then allow yourself peace of mind, focusing on the scent. What is it trying to tell

you? What visions does it inspire? Is there a deity that manifests in your thoughts? Think of an evocative name for your incense. How does it make you feel and of what does it remind you? What memory or emotions does it elicit? Create a story or a poem about your experience. Record your thoughts as memories, as music, or other inspiration. Listen to what the incense is trying to tell you, for the outcome of such reflection is the cultivation of an elegant mind.

Fire is passion. Fire is inspiration. Fire consumes and purifies. It is powerful and dangerous. It attracts and mesmerizes, captivating our imagination. "Playing with fire" infers inviting a dangerous situation; however, the natural magick approach alters this relationship. Fire is playful, it dances and entices and when it is treated with reverence, respect, and caution, the benefits of working with this powerful element are numerous. Just as the hearth fire welcomes and sustains us with its inviting warmth, the rays of the sun have healing energy. Like fire, the sun must also be approached with caution. Too much exposure to its life-giving rays is harmful. One of the outcomes of practicing natural magick is the discovery of the balance point where sufficient benefit is gained and the practitioner remains free from harm.

Chapter Six

WELLS OF EMOTION, RIVERS, AND OCEANS

The Realm of Water

S eventy percent of the earth's surface is covered in water. Similarly, our brain and heart are composed of 73 percent water, and our total body weight is approximately 90 percent water. Water is life, the cradle of existence. Its elemental association is that of the emotional realm. Oceans, rivers, lakes, and streams become metaphors for our inner spiritual lives. Connections in nature are exemplified by the vast network of rivers.

Hans-Henrik Stolum, a former professor of earth sciences at Cambridge University, sought to quantify the world's rivers and made a fascinating discovery. He measured the longest rivers in the world in two ways. First, he measured a direct line from the source of the river to its mouth. Then, he measured the meandering paths that each river took across the earth. What Stolum discovered was that the ratio between these two distances was 1:3.14. This is significant because even the rivers seem to want to move in a circle, to echo the divine pattern that gives rise to the universe. The relationship of 1:3.14 is the same ratio of the diameter of a circle to its circumference. We all live within the borders of a watershed. Rivers were the first roadways; they were the connections between communities, avenues of trade, transportation, and communication. The earliest civilizations of Mesopotamia flourished in the fertile crescent between the Tigris and Euphrates rivers where Ishtar and Inanna were the supreme goddesses of the land. Ishtar, the most important goddess in the Akkadian pantheon, was worshipped in fertility rites as a symbol of pure love, a universal creatrix, and the mother of the gods.

In the power of the oceans, we feel the waves of divinity. Powerful deities such as Tiamat, Poseidon, Yemaya, and Thetis have all been connected to the sea. Life-giving and powerful, water sustains us. Without it, life on earth would not be possible. The veneration of wells was an important ritual practice among ancient pagans. Wells took on a mythical quality as portals into a mystical world. Alternately, they were believed to possess powers that could affect the lives of mortals. Even today, the practice of tossing a coin into a fountain echoes the age-old understanding that from the life-giving presence of water, there is much to be gained and a price to be paid.

Access to fresh potable water is the single most important indicator of survival of a civilization or settlement, and this resource is undeniable in its ability to shape reality. From the gentle rain that nourishes and cleanses, to the unknowable depths of the deepest trenches of the ocean, the wandering paths of rivers, and the quiet stillness of lakes and ponds, the magic of water is all around us.

From the annual flooding of the Nile that gave rise to Egyptian civilization to the sacred Ganges river, which is said to possess healing properties, the element of water has always played a major role in religious expression. Even the Christian sacrament of baptism echoes the pagan tradition in which a person must pass through a stand of water in order to break an enchantment. The lure and lore of water is found in legends of mermaids and selkies, of the lost kingdom of Atlantis, and in the Arthurian legend of the Lady of the Lake, where Excalibur is secreted.

Nereids, The Sea Priestesses

The Greek goddess Thetis, mother of Achilles, was among the most prominent of the nereids. The nereids were the daughters of Nereus and Amphitrite, although in some accounts, the wife of Nereus, Doris, is also attributed to their source. Depicted in ancient texts, the nereids are described as fifty or one hundred individuals who had the ability to interact with sea creatures both real and mythical. They would escort heroes from near death back to life, or from life to immortality. They were featured in celebrations and were described as holding small fish and dolphins, sometimes even carrying armor. They were believed to possess protective powers, and offerings were made to them in exchange for safe passage over the sea.

MEDITATION: OPENING THE LOTUS: A SPIRITUAL AWAKENING

The lotus is a symbol of spiritual enlightenment because of its unique life cycle. The stem and roots are aquatic, completely submerged, while the leaves rest on the surface of the water, and the beautiful blossom appears to float above. The lotus has many petals, each representing an aspect of spirit. The lotus in bloom represents the individual undergoing a spiritual awakening, while the stem and roots remain tethered to the earth. Use this meditation when you are seeking to open your mind to higher levels of consciousness. The image of the lotus can aid you in conceptualizing letting go. The emptying of the mind is a key component to meditation, while still remaining a connection to the water and earth. If it is possible, try to meditate near a body of water to deepen your connection to this element.

- Begin with a basic awareness of your body. Sit in a lotus position, on the ground with your knees crossed and your hands resting on your knees with your palms facing up. Focus at first on your heartbeat. Listen for it and feel it. When you begin to get in sync with the natural rhythm of your heartbeat, begin to slowly and purposefully inhale through your nose to a count of four heartbeats. Hold the breath for four heartbeats and exhale for the same duration. When you have exhaled, wait four heartbeats before you inhale again. Get into a deep and steady pattern as you breathe in on a count of four, hold for four, exhale for four, and hold your breath for four counts again. This is all determined by the rhythm of your heart. Get in touch with your natural rhythm as you envision a seed.
- It is a rich brown oval, an earthy ellipse, smooth and dark, about the color of a coffee bean. Its outer casing keeps it merrily floating along a tranquil body of water. The seed is buoyant. It bobs along peacefully. Take some time to envision the water. Ask yourself, is it a river? A lake? A pond? Where has your desire transported you? You are on a journey to awaken your highest spiritual self, and you begin in sacred water.

- The waters are pulled by the moon; slowly you watch as they recede. The seed sinks into the soft silt and mud. There it rests to await the return of the waters. A season passes. You observe the silent passage of time. The waters begin to return. Throughout this time the seed has remained protected in depths of the supple earth. Now, the growing season has begun. You watch as the seed bursts forth with life, sending a lush green shoot up toward the surface of the returning waters, simultaneously sending white roots into the yielding silt and sediment below.

- You feel this power in your own body. You are linked to this process of growth and awakening. The exploration of the root bed is easy as a network of roots feel their way through the layers below. Radiating growth in both directions, the green shoot breaks the surface of the water above. Like a graceful spiral unfolding, a large circular leaf begins to unfurl. It is rough along the bottom, heavily textured with thick veins that run along its underside. A beautiful pattern emerges, almost like a spiderweb that radiates outward from a central point. You are looking up at the leaf from below. You notice how the edges of the leaf curl upward, creating a protective shelf. Your spirit moves freely, and you can observe above and below. You are at one with the water, and you observe the beauty of the life that it supports all around you. Birds flock to it. Fish swim in it. And before your eyes, a beautiful blossom begins to open. Its petals are white, and layer upon layer of harmonious perfume is released into the air, attracting all manner of life. Scarab beetles, the sacred symbol of the sun, find secret chambers within.

- With each opening petal, a new dimension of peace is revealed to you. Like the lotus, you float above the plane of reality that keeps you anchored as well. You exist in many worlds at once: the riverbed, the water itself, and the air above. You are witness to this miraculous manifestation of life, and you experience it internally as well. You see the lotus as a facet of your spiritual awakening, for now you observe that it is possible to occupy several planes of existence at once, to be both above and below, to be a source of beauty in the world, to be connected to the earth and provide shelter for its creatures. You take these lessons of the lotus into your spirit, for they are nature's gift to you.

HERBAL RITUAL BATH

A ritual bath may be taken at any time, but it is particularly useful before a sacred rite such as initiation or ordination. Our planet is a water planet, and a ritual bath gives the natural magick practitioner another way to connect with the divine elemental energies of water. You will choose dried herbs that suit your purpose, be it preparation or dedication, and you will combine your herbs with other elements to create a meditative and cleansing ritual.

You will need:

- A drawstring muslin pouch.
- One half-cup of sea salt. Be mindful when choosing your salt. Consider its origin, as this element can work as a symbolic link to a specific geographic area.
- One cup of magnesium sulfate mineral salts (Epsom salts).
- One quarter-cup of dried herbs. Choose with intention and outcome in mind. Popular ingredients include lavender (calming), mint (stimulating), and rosemary (for remembrance).
- Three to five drops of a harmonizing essential oil, can be of the same variety of the herbs.
- A clean, dry glass jar for mixing and storage.
- A screen for the drain if performing the ritual bath indoors in a tub.
- An essential oil blend of your own making to resonate with your purpose.

Directions:

1. Begin by combining the dry ingredients in the jar. Mix them together well by shaking the jar or by turning it over and over. Add the drops of essential oil, five if you are using a single oil and

three of each if you are using a combination. Shake again to distribute the oil throughout the salt mixture. Fill the muslin pouch with the mixture. The rest can be stored for later use.

2. Prepare yourself mentally for the ritual bath by stating to yourself what it is that you wish to accomplish. As earlier stated, this ritual can be done as preparation before a greater rite such as a rite of passage or formal Sabbat. Ritual baths are particularly helpful for priestesses and ritual facilitators who will benefit from the extra level of preparation before expending the energy on the greater ritual. Think about the level and type of attunement that you seek. Create an essential oil blend as described in Chapter 4 that will serve your purpose and augment your energy. You can use the same herbal properties in the ritual bath.

3. Begin by using your oil blend to anoint your forehead, inner wrists, and the bottoms of your feet. Next, begin running a hot bath. Hang the muslin pouch around the faucet so that the hot water flows through and dissolves the salts. You may darken the room and light it with candles to enhance your experience. If you like, you can also sprinkle some dried herbs directly into the bath water. If you choose to do so, be sure to use a screen or strainer over the drain so as not to create any plumbing clogs when your bath is over.

4. When the tub is filled, get in and breathe deeply, taking in the aroma of the bath. Hold your breath, close your eyes, and completely submerge yourself. Contemplate the work ahead and project yourself into that future space by envisioning the best possible outcomes. Before a ritual of importance, it is not unusual for an obstacle to manifest. Think of the ways you can use this place of relaxation and peace to overcome any challenges that may arise. Remember the sacred willow tree that seeks that water's edge: strong and flexible, you must make your plans carefully but be prepared to switch gears at any moment.

5. A ritual bath can help fortify your spirit and amplify your energy so that you may radiate it forth to others. Allow yourself to remain in the bath as long as it takes you to focus or until the water grows

tepid and is no longer comfortable. When you step out, repeat the five-point anointing and prepare yourself for the tasks at hand.

Indicium Aquae: "The Swimming Test"

The connection between witches and water has a tragic component. The *indicium aquae*, or "swimming test," was used in the Middle Ages (and sometimes later) to determine if a person was guilty of practicing witchcraft. The Scottish witchcraft act, Anentis Witchcraftis, was enacted by the Protestant Scottish parliament on June 4, 1563, during the reign of the Catholic Mary, Queen of Scots. A similar law was passed in England in January 1563, making witchcraft illegal across the British Isles. The Scottish law was the harsher of the two; not only was witchcraft prohibited, but the state of being of a witch was a crime punishable by death. In England, acts of witchcraft were forbidden, and punishment was tiered according to the severity of the offense. Witchcraft itself was never explicitly defined, and in Scotland, the knowledge of or seeking out of witchcraft was also punishable by death. A person accused of witchcraft would be bound up and thrown into water that had been blessed. If the water "rejected" the accused, she would float to the surface and was subsequently found guilty. If the accused sank to the bottom and drowned, she was presumed to be innocent of the charges. The Anentis Witchcraftis was not repealed until 1736. An estimated two thousand people were executed for crimes, including sorcery, charms, enchantments, invocations, and conjuration during this time.

SPELL: AQUA VITALIS SPIRITUAL BLESSING

One of the cardinal elementals, water has a vast association with magick of many kinds. Aside from the practical applications such as washing and cleansing, the ritual use of water has been employed to achieve everything from spiritual purity and apotropaic magick to blessings and expressions of gratitude. Water can be used for scrying, purification, and the pouring of a libation into the earth. How you choose to use water in your magick will be determined by your geographical area and your magickal goals. Whether you are practicing alone or with a group, using water to perform a spiritual blessing serves as a reminder of our physical dependency on water, the necessity of water to nourish the land, and its association with mystery.

Water Witching

Water witching, also known as dowsing, is the process of locating underground water sources through unexplained sensory perception. Dowsing is also referred to as "water divining." Dowsing is a way of gathering information from the environment. Minute changes in the electromagnetic field of energy caused by the movement of underground water can also reveal the presence of mineral deposits. The earliest reference to prospecting for minerals is Georgius Agricola's *De Re Metallica*, published in 1556. It is very interesting to note that the concept of "divining" for water involves acute sensory perception in the practitioner. Often, tools such as pendulums or rods are used to detect underground water. These tools will respond to changes in the environment that would otherwise be undetectable. By keeping a conduit in a state of both balance and tension, the natural magick practitioner is better able to detect the subtle changes in energy and thus be able to divine information from the unseen environment.

Water is symbolic of the emotions; it is constantly in flux. Water is mutable and takes on many forms. It can be frozen as ice, liquid as water, evaporated as steam, and it has the ability to condense its nature and create a cyclical energy that sustains life on the planet. We are inextricably linked to water. Water partly composes us, and without it we cannot survive. This spell is designed to acknowledge and amplify our connection to water in a metaphysical sense. It is a symbolic recognition of the power of water and how it shapes our perception. It can be done indoors or outdoors, solitary or with a group.

You will need:

- A chalice full of water
- A small sea sponge
- A circle of white cloth, around five inches in diameter; choose a natural fabric such as cotton
- A blue cord (yarn or thread will work) to bind up the cloth

Directions:

1. Put the sea sponge on the circle of fabric, gather up the edges toward the center, and tie them together with the cord. Soak the wrapped sponge in the chalice of water to saturate it. Squeeze off some of the excess so that it is not overly drippy. Hold it over your third eye and take a moment to experience the coolness and moisture. Close your eyes and imagine yourself looking over a vast sea as you say these words:

   "Water is mystery; its depths unknowable.
   I ask for the power of seeing beyond, that these mysteries become
   revealed to me, that I may work in harmony with this
   most necessary and vital element. So mote it be."

2. Place the wrapped sponge back into the chalice and repeat the saturation and expelling of water. Touch the bundle to your lips and breathe deeply. Notice if there is any scent you can discern. Think of how the water feels upon your lips. Close your eyes and imagine that you are looking over a crystal clear, cold spring. Intone these words:

   "Life-giving waters that do sustain us, bring me your gift of clarity.
   May your stillness inspire me to choose careful words, to speak truth
   with confidence, and to share the blessings of your inspiration so that I
   may show forth your power in my work. So mote it be."

3. Replenish the sponge by returning it to the chalice and repeating the action, only this time you will hold it in the center of your chest, beneath your clothing (unless your practice is skyclad) so that it rests against your skin. For your third intonation you will envision a turbulent river.

   "Wild and powerful, sacred waters will flow where they will.
   I invoke the force of passion, the strength that can wear away
   solid stone. In the rushing currents, I attune the beating of

*my heart. My blood flows energetically, full of life and vitality.
I ask for comfort amidst the uncontrollable, for inner peace
within turbulence. All this I seek, so mote it be."*

If you are using this threefold blessing as part of a coven ritual, it should be carried out so that all participants perform each blessing in succession (i.e., the chalice would be passed around as each practitioner performs the third eye blessing). At the conclusion of each blessing, the companion would leave the wrapped sponge in the chalice and pass it to the next person until the chalice makes its way around the circle three times.

AQUA VITAE APOTHECARY: MAKING HERBAL TINCTURES

In medieval times, distilled spirits were believed to have magical potency. The distillation of alcohol is credited to Taddeo Alderotti, an Italian doctor, scholar, and alchemist who lived from c. 1205 until 1295. Alcohol is both an astringent and a preservative and is a necessary component to creating tinctures, which are liquid extracts containing an essence of herbs, roots, bark, or flowers. Often used in medicine, herbal tinctures can also be used for spiritual strengthening.

Perhaps no one has understood this more completely than Edward Bach, who created a system of remedies known as the Bach Flower Remedies. Bach's philosophy was built on the understanding that in its glory and simplicity, the healing power of nature was not limited to the physical body. Bach created a series of remedies meant to address more esoteric concerns. By combining herbage steeped or boiled in "rock water," or pure spring water that flows from the earth, with brandy, he created a method of addressing afflictions of the spirit such as specific fears, feelings of anxiety, preoccupation, oversensitivity, loneliness, jealousy, the inability to live in the present moment, and other forms of despondency. By embracing the beauty and subtle effects that magick confers upon those who practice it, it is possible to elevate your spiritual vibration and improve your metal state.

Dr. Bach used recognizable and easily obtainable ingredients in his remedies and was so generous of spirit that he published his methods, making the remedies and their creation available to any who wished to experience them. Remedies using honeysuckle, wild rose, olive, mustard, impatiens, agrimony, centaury, walnut, holly, pine, elm, willow, and oak were all included in his body of work devoted to improving the mental state and consequently the overall health of the practitioners who availed themselves of his knowledge. The natural magick practitioner will notice several sacred and magic-bearing plants in this partial list. Creating your own tinctures is a powerful way to harness the energy of nature and use it to transform your life. How you plan to use your tinctures and which ingredients you choose to include will be determined by your own needs and expectations. Different types of herbage (woody or leafy, fresh or dried) will require slightly different preparation methods. The general method of preparation is as follows.

You will need:

- A clean, sterilized glass jar with a tight-fitting lid, one jar for each extract you plan to create
- Eighty- to ninety-proof vodka
- Grain alcohol, 190 proof
- Herbs (fresh or dried), berries, or flowers with which you have chosen to work
- A funnel
- Cheesecloth
- Dark glass or amber bottles with droppers

Directions:

1. Begin by preparing your herbal material. Whether you are using fresh or dried, everything will need to be very finely chopped, as fine as possible. Fill your sterilized jar about halfway with the herbs if you are using dried plant material. Then, fill the jar to the very top with vodka, making sure all plant material is completely

covered. If you are using fresh herbs, more will be needed because it is more difficult to extract from moist material. Tear the leaves and stems and pack them into the jar. Press down and add more until the jar is very full.

2. While vodka works very well as a preservative and an astringent, sometimes a stronger extracting solution is needed. This can be done by making a solution with a 1:1 ratio using equal parts of the vodka and the grain alcohol. Make sure the herbs are covered completely and fill the jar to the top.

3. If there is cultural tradition or a condition that prohibits you from using alcohol of any kind, it is possible to make nonalcoholic tinctures using vinegar or glycerin. While not as effective as alcohol because these ingredients are not as strong, they will still work; however, these preparations are more prone to spoilage, so extra attentive care will need to be taken. Never use rubbing alcohol or denatured alcohol. These will not work. You must use ethyl alcohol, the type used for drinking. Do not use flavored alcohols. Vodka or brandy are the most appropriate choices.

4. Store the jars away from light and heat, in a cool, dark cupboard and check on them weekly. Each week, shake the jars gently for a few minutes and check to make certain that the alcohol has not evaporated. If you see evidence of evaporation, open the jars and refill them to the top, making sure the plant material is submerged. Exposure to air can ruin a tincture, so you want to be very observant of this. After storing the tinctures for six to eight weeks, you may strain off the liquid.

5. Drape the cheesecloth over the funnel and place the funnel in the amber bottle. Pour off the liquid and fill as many bottles as you can. You can even add the saturated herbs to the cheesecloth and express any remaining extract through the cloth. Make sure to label your tinctures with the ingredients you chose and the date on which they were prepared. Since alcohol is both a solvent and a preservative, the tinctures will last for many years. You can add a few drops to your ritual bath for an enhanced connection to nature.

HERBAL CHARM: MAKING AN AROMATHERAPY SPRAY

There is much emphasis on the preparation of ritual space, as it creates a vibration of ritual participants truly being between the worlds. Aromatherapy is another method of creating a bond between the natural world and your physical space. Aromatherapy can be used as part of the preparation for ritual, to enhance a meditation, or even for daily use to bring about harmonious states of balance and peace. Creating your own aromatherapy spray allows you to engage the water element with your growing knowledge of herbs and your skills at blending their essential oils into an essence that can stimulate creativity or change the energy of a physical place in order to attune it to the work at hand.

You will need:

- One and one-half ounces of distilled water
- One quarter-ounce of witch hazel
- Fifteen to twenty drops of an essential oil blend
- A dark-colored glass bottle with a spray top, capable of holding two ounces
- A shot glass or other glass to blend your oils
- A small funnel to transfer the essential oil blend into the suspension

Directions:

1. In the small glass, combine a carrier oil such as jojoba or fractionated coconut oil with your choice of essential oils to suit your purpose. Remember that even though you are creating a suspension in distilled water, you must still follow all the steps for creating the essential oil blend by balancing base, middle, and top notes. You may also create a simple aromatherapy spray using a single essential oil if you wish; however, the essential oil must still be diluted with a carrier. Create the blend or dilute a simple oil and set it aside.

2. Carefully use the funnel to pour the distilled water and the witch hazel into the bottle. Add the oil blend to the bottle and screw on the top. Shake the mixture to blend it. Your aromatherapy spray is now ready to use. It should be stored in a cool, dry place away from light and heat. Use the spray liberally whenever you are in need of a pick-me-up. You can also listen to the fragrance and create an evocative and esoteric name for it based on the herbal properties you chose to create it.

WATERS OF FORTUNE SPELL FOR PROSPERITY

Collect nine silver coins, either silver dollars, or quarters and half-dollars minted before 1964. These will have a silver content of 90 percent. Place them in a small bowl or shallow dish and cover them with spring water. Allow the bowl to charge in the moonlight by exposing it to the rays of the full moon. Touch your fingers into the water and with them anoint your forehead, your hands, and anything that will assist you in connection with your effort as you speak the words:

"I accept the prosperity that is rightly mine.
I reject scarcity in its deceptive guise. I welcome abundance,
as it comes right soon. I give thanks by the light of a bountiful moon.
May fair Fortuna smile on me, my fate blessed by the warm
and welcoming sea. By the power of three times three,
as I will so mote it be."

Continue the incantations until the efficacy of your spell is evident.

Using water in magickal ways is empowering to the natural magick practitioner. Acknowledging our connection to water and using it for magickal purposes creates a deeper understanding of the subtle transformational powers of water. Water is perhaps the most mutable of all the elements. It connects us to our origin in a particular way. It is also receptive and reacts to the environment.

The Japanese author, photographer, and doctor of alternative medicine Masaru Emoto dedicated a huge body of his work to photographing and cataloging how water crystals form under particular circumstances. He found that water will react and form either beautiful and ordered or chaotic and disordered crystals depending on the type of stimuli to which it is exposed. In his photographic works, water crystals gathered from the source of a river or downstream from a source reveal beautiful and ordered patterns that follow divine proportion and sacred geometry. Water crystals gathered from water that had been dammed, its flow inhibited, show a disrupted, inconsistent, and irregular arrangement. Similarly, water crystals grown in the presence of nature tend to reflect the beauty of natural order.

Even more intriguing is photographic evidence that when the water crystals are exposed to kind words and positive emotions, their crystalline structure mimics this harmony. The opposite is also true: water crystals grown amidst negative sentiments show the irregularities observed in inhibited or polluted water. Emoto's work seems to suggest that the element of water has a certain sentience about it. It responds, reacts, and is greatly changed by its environment. The sentience of water is something to be considered when using, conserving, and respecting this powerful life-giving element.

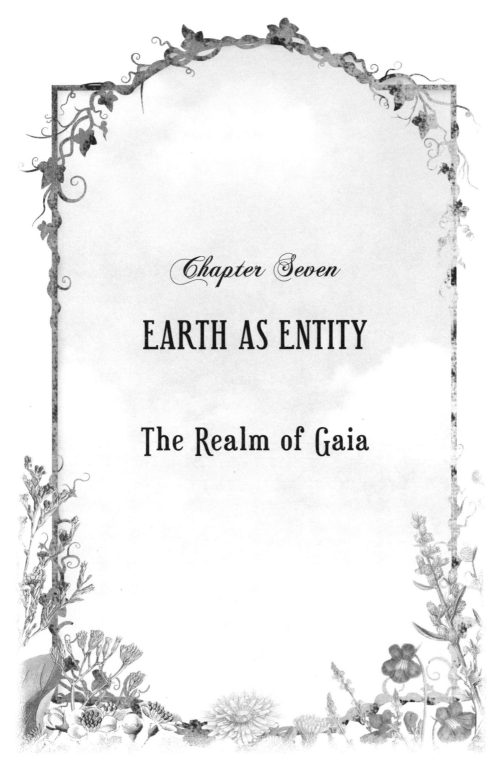

Chapter Seven

EARTH AS ENTITY

The Realm of Gaia

An evolving body of thought over the past several decades views the earth as a single living being. This single living being is made up of the vast network of interactions among all species that inhabit the earth. This concept, called Gaia Theory or the Gaia Hypothesis, grew out of an idea created by R. Buckminster Fuller, who described the earth as a spaceship upon which we are passengers. Other scientists, such as James Lovelock, have expounded upon this theory, suggesting that life on earth regulates itself. Amateur archaeologist and avid photographer Alfred Watkins was the first to describe what would later become known as "ley lines": a complex system of energetic pathways that traverse the planet.

However different the disciplines from which these concepts arose, they are all rooted in a common belief that the earth is a powerful being, capable of self-healing and awareness. The earth contains energy centers that humans are not readily able to perceive. The applications to natural magick lie in accepting ourselves as an integral part of the whole. When we cast a circle, we are actually creating an energetic field of power. "Ley hunters," the name given to people who enthusiastically seek and plot ley lines, are also tapping into an energetic awareness. Dowsers, too, use subtle energies to locate unseen deposits of minerals and water. And throughout the planet, we observe the symbiosis between different types of organisms, including ourselves.

The Gaia of classical mythology was a force to be reckoned with. The mother of the Titans, Gaia was creatrix and protector. Born from Chaos, she gave birth to the heavens by herself alone. She brought forth the mountains and the sea, giving form to what we experience as the physical world. She is the source of all nourishment, the embodiment of earth in all its power. Her worship is older than that of the Olympian gods, and she is credited with being the mother of the elements and the cosmos. To invoke Gaia is to attune to the "oneness" of life on earth. Within her dwell all creatures of the air, land, and sea. In natural magick, bonds between organic and inorganic entities are cultivated. Relationships to spirit animals, familiars, herbs, rocks, crystals, and other minerals enhance the effects of working natural magick. In the realm of Gaia, we explore the mystery of ley lines, the wisdom of animals, the power of minerals, and the different ways we psychically impact our environment through casting circles and raising cones of power. Beyond life on earth, there is life *in* earth— in the unseen depths—as well as in the spaces above and below and in between the visible and tangible workings of the world. As you explore deeply, be prepared to expand your horizons and open yourself to ideas beyond what you believed possible.

A MAGICKAL NETWORK: VISUALIZING LEY LINES

In the early part of the twentieth century, the concept of ley lines was introduced to the world by Alfred Watkins. In photographic journals of his field work, he found an interesting correlation between natural monuments and the placement of standing stones, churches, and wells. Intrigued, Watkins began plotting lines on maps in between significant natural features. Inevitably, he discovered manmade marking points in between. His hypothesis was that these were the early pathways of ancient people, trading routes that arose from the need of natural resources located farther than the eye could see. In fact, as an amateur archaeologist, Watkins would often find evidence of his hypothesis when following the markers in between land formations.

This harmonic alignment between the natural world and what Watkins assumed was the manipulation of the terrain by prehistoric people provided a fascinating jumping-off point for a new kind of natural magick. Were these points simply a way to map out paths in between sites, a simple visual overland navigational tool, or was there more to it? A fascination with the old trackways captured the imagination of others who presumed that these ley lines were perhaps energetic centers radiating from deep within the earth, and that the markers were intentionally placed there in order to record and acknowledge high-energy places. In between natural sighting points such as the peaks of hills were secondary points, made with clear purpose. These places gathered an aura of power about them, or perhaps the power was there to begin with and the marker simply acknowledged the power.

Whatever the case, Watkins discovered a consistent pattern. The secondary sighting points would sometimes take the form of a lone tree planted on top of a mound of earth, or a sacred well. The markers were either earth, water, stone, or tree. The high ground featured markers of earth while the low ground markers were water, sometimes a moat. And interestingly, at places where the trackways crossed, there was often a castle or a church. At the low marker points, there was usually a homestead. Those investigating and mapping the lines had a growing sense that there was more to these places than just old trading paths. The belief that ley lines were a natural product of the earth, a network of connected energetic pathways that arose from deep within the earth, began to bloom. Even Watkins mused about the possibility that the ley lines were somehow connected with witchcraft:

"The fact of the ley, with its highly skilled technical methods, being established, it must also be a fact that such work required skilled men, carefully trained. Men of knowledge they would be, and therefore men of power over the common people. And now comes surmise. Did they make their craft a mystery to others as ages rolled by? Were they a learned and priestly class, not admitted until completing a long training— as Caesar describes the Druids? Or did they—as Diodorus and Strabo says of Druids—become also bards and soothsayers? Did they, as the ley decayed, degenerate into the witches of the middle ages? Folk-lore provides the witches with the power of riding through the air on a broomstick, the power of overlooking, that of the evil eye. They (in imagination) flew over the Broomy Hills and the Brom-leys. It may be that the ancient sighting methods were condemned as sorcery by the early Christian missionaries."

The study of ley lines originated in Great Britain, but investigators quickly moved beyond the boundaries of the United Kingdom.

Ley hunters took the techniques from England and began to apply them to their own regions.

The identification of ley lines began with a map. First, two natural topographical features, significant enough to warrant mapping, would be located. Historical maps are well suited to this use, as they often contain information regarding water sources and place names that suggest a ley line. Place names that contain suffixes such as mount, cross, and bury are examples. In Great Britain, a portion of the famed St. Michael's ley line creates a perfect right triangle with Glastonbury and Avebury and the standing stones of Stonehenge. Furthermore, Watkins refers to several points noted on a map of Taylor's County from 1757 named Cross Oak, Cross Colloe, and Cross Ash. Watkins originally believed these points to be church crosses until he discovered they were actually the sites of real trees that marked the intersection of ley lines—the point where two ley lines crossed. Historic maps are the primary source documents for the plotting of ley lines because they often contain references to significant natural features that might not be noted on current iterations. A map with a one-to-one inch-to-mile ratio is preferred. Once you have identified two natural features on the map, it is time for field work. Using a compass, try to find a marker between the two points. The distance between points in a ley can be fifty to sixty miles long. The markers would be within those two points, at about a ten- or twenty- or thirty-mile mark, depending on the original distance between two points. When investigating between points, look for manmade markers such as a burial mound or a secondary point such as a pond. Since water has a reflective element, it makes an excellent sighting point between feature points.

Watkins also discovered that historically named trees often occurred at the midpoints, or the crossing points, of ley lines. Gospel Oaks, Kind's Acre Elm, Eastwood Oak, Lyde Cross Tree, Cross Ash, and Hazel Cross Tree are but a few. In many cases, these places named for trees turned out to be the actual places where these named trees once stood. Note that each of the historically named trees found at the crossing points of ley lines are all also part of the canon of venerated trees from antiquity. The mystique of these points of power increased over the centuries. People believed them to be much more than just

The Modern Witchcraft Book of Natural Magick

primitive signposts and maps. Ley centers were and still are thought to be points of underground energy. Stone markers were strategically placed on top of the energy centers to draw the deep earth energy up to the surface. It is also interesting to note that ley lines occur at different levels. There are ley lines at sea level and at varying altitudes. They are perceived as the "thought lines" of the earth and are not considered part of reality as we normally perceive it.

Ley Lines and Science

Western science does not recognize the electromagnetic energy associated with ley lines. In order to qualify as reality, objective science demands that all energetic output should be measurable and repeatable. This stricture prohibits all unexplained phenomena from valid recognition and does not account for intuition or personal gnosis.

When you visualize ley lines, whether you believe you have located them on an ordinance or historic map or intuited them through feeling or perhaps even discovered field evidence as Alfred Watkins did, think of the lines according to their respective heights and depths. They radiate from within the earth and vibrate at frequencies that sensitive souls are able to detect. At their crossing point, they form a network of powerful energy. Visualize the earth generating and being held safe within a net made up of electromagnetically charged threads. They surround the earth, they permeate it, and they hover in the atmosphere. Visualize your place along the ley lines and see yourself as an integral part of the network, a beneficial being devoted to magick, to protecting and healing the earth and honoring her sacred places. You may even find a special grove for your next ritual or get an affirmation of your attunement to the energies of the deep earth.

MEDITATION: IDENTIFYING YOUR SPIRIT ANIMAL

Contained within the bounty, beauty, and power of the earth are all the creatures that instruct us on the elements of our primal nature. Animals and plants live in a harmonious balance with the earth that humans cannot approach. We cannot seem to function without altering our environment. While trees and birds and the creatures of the forest have all discovered how to survive and thrive solely in the context of nature, we are compelled to alter our environment to suit our unique needs.

Practicing natural magick provides the opportunity to observe and integrate the wisdom of the natural world. Approaching the natural world with magickal intention requires honesty and intuition. In magick, intuition is accepted as an inner wisdom. There is no external system for validating a magickal experience. Intuition is aligned with truth and is centered in nature and within our nature as individuals. Nurturing the connection to nature takes diligence and practice.

Animals have this ability without any instruction. They rely on instinct and intuition. When we seek to gain wisdom from animals, it is beneficial to study their mystical attributes and what the animals energetically represent to people. In the indigenous American tradition, there are fifty-two circles of animal wisdom. To find your spirit animals, you will choose from an unknown array. You can easily draw the pattern although it will take some time. Visualize a large circle. Along the circumference of the circle are fifty-two small circles. You can create the diagram on a large sheet of white paper, using a dime as a template to trace the smaller circles. Then, select nine of the circles at random; this centers the energy of intuition. After the random selection of nine circles is made, give each circle a number, one through fifty-two beginning at the bottom and then going sunwise around the circle. Each numbered circle corresponds with a different spirit animal. Each animal will have a different attribute or spiritual significance. To locate your nine spirit animals, write down the numbers assigned to each of the nine chosen circles and then check them against this list. You will only need to do this once, and make sure to record your results in your grimoire. You can learn so much from spirit animals.

1. **Ant:** Representing communication, the ants create pathways. They are earth movers and are adept at working together. Ant magick is indicative of a stable and sustainable way of life.
2. **Antelope:** The antelope represents the skill of listening. To awaken your listening ability is to engage in clear thinking.

With listening comes harmony and peace that will resonate through your core.

3. **Armadillo:** The armadillo is representative of grounding and protection. The armadillo is finely tuned in to its environment, able to detect false movements that hinder freedom. When you are in need of boundaries, the energy of the armadillo will come to your aid.

4. **Badger:** The badger has a centering energy. When changes are on the horizon, it is the badger that will warn others of impending danger. The badger is representative of the gift of perception.

5. **Bat:** With its gift of inner sight, the ability to echolocate, and fly by night, the bat represents the principled mind. Bats have the energetic quality of fearlessness. They unite the land and the sky.

6. **Bear:** The bear survives the cold of winter and teaches us the value of promises fulfilled. After suffering through the cold, the bear emerges to springtime and fulfills the lessons of survival.

7. **Beaver:** Representing survival, ingenuity, and transformation, the beaver redefines its landscape. The beaver assures its own survival through use of its skills and instinct. Few are able to command the forces of the swirling rivers like the beaver.

8. **Bee:** The bee is the emblem of perseverance, and it is character-ized by work and diligence. The reward for such perseverance is the sweet gift of honey. Behind every triumph is a concentrated effort. The sweetness comes into being through work.

9. **Buffalo:** Stamina is the lesson of the buffalo. When scarcity strikes, the buffalo represent sacrifice, selflessness, and gracious giving. They do not give up. They do what is required, relocat-ing if necessary.

10. **Butterfly:** Resplendent in its beauty, the butterfly signifies the gift of enchantment and transformation. One of the few crea-tures that complete metamorphosis, the butterfly emerges from threads of life woven into a sacred space.

11. **Chicken:** The chicken represents sociability. After hatching, chickens will huddle together to keep warm, creating bonds through touch. Their feathers arrive, blanketing them with

warmth. Frequent eaters, chickens are believed to transform food into love.

12. **Cow:** Solemnity is the lesson of the cow. A symbol of strength and resourcefulness, the cow is revered for its beautiful eyes. The cow is also expected to give its milk for creatures other than its own young. Since cows only produce milk when there are baby calves to nurse, the cows are separated from their young; hence their sadness.

13. **Coyote:** A cunning forager, the coyote's gift is humor. The lesson of the coyote is to learn how to balance wants and needs and still find time for play. The energetic coyote will leap and follow whatever catches its eye.

14. **Crow:** The laws of the earth and the domain of remembrance are the hallmarks of the crow. A messenger of peace, the crow manifests to remind us of our reasons for living. The true centering light is rooted in love.

15. **Deer:** The skillful deer is the great runner. Gentle and without aggression, the deer is hunted by many and must rely on its skills and speed to survive. The deer represents clarity of mind and strength in body.

16. **Dog:** The loyal dog is among the oldest of domesticated creatures. Dogs represent brotherhood and devotion. Descendants of wolves, they live among humans as family and teach the importance of bonds and loyalty.

17. **Dolphin:** The dolphin is the keeper of the sacred breath and represents the essence of clarity. With uncanny intelligence and highly developed communication skills, the dolphin is among the most revered of water creatures.

18. **Dragonfly:** Illumination is the gift of the dragonfly. Its body symbolizes trust through stability. It possesses four wings, the upper two representing peace and love, the lower wings symbolizing cause and effect.

19. **Eagle:** The messenger of peace, the eagle soars into an endless sky, inspiring all that behold its power, beauty, and strength. A bringer of mystery, the eagle is among the most significant of the winged creatures and represents transcendent knowledge.

20. **Elk:** Representing balance, the elk teaches us to counter the effects of fear and doubt with skills and talents. Able to survive in the face of the elements, the elk also expands the qualities of the deer, being the larger member of the family.

21. **Fox:** Cunning and camouflage are the gifts of the fox. Led by mysterious forces, the fox learns how to be elusive and blend in with its surroundings. Able to perceive the unseen, the fox is a teacher of wisdom.

22. **Frog:** Maturity is the lesson of the frog. Like the butterfly, the frog begins life as one creature and leaves the former self in the past to fulfill its destiny. The frog reminds us to bring ideas into reality and to be ready to part with old patterns that no longer serve our needs.

23. **Goat:** A creature that can balance on different terrains, the goat is surefooted and adventurous. Call upon the energy of the goat when you need to navigate difficulty with a sense of confidence and bravery.

24. **Grouse:** The grouse brings us the joy of the dance. Expressions of joy and the sacred spiral dance of healing and restoration reinforce feelings of peace. The grouse teaches us to address hurt and to bring healing and joy wherever we can.

25. **Hawk:** Respect is commanded by the hawk. The most efficient of the sky hunters, the hawk is also a messenger like the eagle. Hawks demand that we respect life. They are also the protectors of travelers.

26. **Heron:** The heron teaches the benefits of spiritual and physical fertility. In order to help the earth mother reproduce her gifts, we must plant the seeds for growing. The heron encourages us to awaken from a dream state and make contributions to inner knowing.

27. **Horse:** Strong, able, and devoted, the horse represents responsibility. The horse has been a leader, a transporter, and a value to mankind. When their numbers are plentiful, they must seek new grounds for grazing in order to survive. Theirs is the gift of direction.

28. **Hummingbird:** The beautiful and swift hummingbird represents energy. Of all the winged creatures, they fly among the

fastest. Appearing to hover suspended in the air, their flight is a wonder to behold. Consult the hummingbird during times of great energetic creation.

29. **Lizard:** The lizard is a dreamer and can be found occupying places of peace. The lizard represents memory. It appears sometimes in dark and lonely places. Lizard energy encourages a meditative state where dreams may enter and forgotten memories are recalled.

30. **Lynx:** Logic and self-awareness are the attributes associated with the lynx. Awareness is cultivated; knowledge can be learned. The lynx sleeps cradled in the boughs of the Tree of Wisdom, a source of spiritual healing.

31. **Moose:** The spirit of the moose creates balance in living. Representing judgment, the moose encourages us to be discerning and not to blindly follow leaders. The proper instinct is to look for reason and follow judgment with wisdom.

32. **Mountain Lion:** Even a leader will need leadership at some point. When the need is clear, consult the energy of the mountain lion. No matter the amount of fear that surrounds you, there is a modicum of peace that is always within reach.

33. **Mouse:** The mouse represents bravery and perseverance. A mouse will travel anywhere and will defend itself vigorously against much larger creatures. Watch a mouse as it forages for food, and you will see a creature that faces fear at every turn yet never gives up.

34. **Opossum:** Diversion is the tactic of the opossum. A cunning actor, the opossum will perform in order to protect itself. Comfortable in its environment, the opossum moves by night in safety. When it is discovered, it will play dead. The skill of the opossum is listening.

35. **Otter:** The otter is recognized for its playful nature. It brings the gift of enthusiasm. With energetic fun and joy, otters were believed to be the first creatures to recognize the heartbeat of the natural world. To this sacred rhythm, they dance.

36. **Owl:** The owl is the voice of wisdom and represents questioning. Even its distinct call sounds like an inquiry. The owl speaks

The Modern Witchcraft Book of Natural Magick

for itself. A talented, swift, and silent hunter, the owl is formidable and wise, different from all other creatures.

37. **Porcupine:** Living close to the earth, the porcupine represents faith. Thoughts are energetic forms that represent who we want to become. This vision is embodied in the porcupine, who appears just as it wants to appear. The porcupine is also ready to defend itself, even at a distance. Use the energy of the porcupine when you most need to believe in yourself.

38. **Rabbit:** The rabbit is a strategist. Elusive and fast, the rabbit will outrun the wolf. Burrowing in the ground, it remains safe and hidden. Knowing when to run and when to withdraw are the keys to its survival. Always chased, the rabbit is adept at strategy and self-preservation.

39. **Raccoon:** Living in groups, the raccoon brings the energy of protection. Intelligent and innovative, it makes sure its family crosses hazardous places in safety. Raccoons' living spaces are communal and they look out for each other.

40. **Raven:** The raven represents change. Like many other winged creatures, the raven is seen as a messenger. The presence of the raven is a warning that change is on the horizon. Listen with patience and truth.

41. **Sheep:** The sheep brings the wisdom of companionship. Among the first livestock, sheep gather in numbers and move from place to place in a surefooted and peaceful manner. Sheep are non-aggressive. Their teaching is that of building peaceful community.

42. **Skunk:** Gentle is the skunk, who is protected by its own impurity. The skunk teaches us that such gentleness cannot exist without some kind of protection, however unpleasant it may be. The skunk is gentle and yet commands great respect.

43. **Snake:** The snake is the emblem of transformation and inner self-love. The snake possesses grounding energy and is thought to be so filled with love and wisdom that it can renew itself from within. The snake teaches the art of releasing.

44. **Snipe:** Discipline is the gift of the snipe. At home along the water and in the sky, the snipe blends in with its surroundings. When they walk, their heads bob down, suggesting humility.

The snipe teaches us to be secure in our appearance and to not be so influenced by the thoughts of others.

45. **Spider:** The spider is the great networker who spins a web of radiance. Stronger than the wind, the web of the spider was among the earliest inspirations for basket weaving. The web it creates is a working tool. It is both a home and a means of survival, a hunting tactic.

46. **Squirrel:** The squirrel is the gatherer. Even if they cannot remember where they have buried their winter stores, nothing is lost. The gathered seeds will become plants or food for other creatures. The squirrel benefits all beings.

47. **Swan:** Gracefully gliding upon mirrorlike waters, the swan is the embodiment of grace. Use the teaching of the swan to recognize the gift of grace that lives within you. There is never a need to seek it elsewhere. True beauty radiates from within.

48. **Turkey:** The turkey is concerned with image and outward appearance. Its plumage grants it a place of recognition and honor, and its feathers are used for ceremonies. The turkey is also a messenger of peace.

Skin Turning and Familiars

Familiars, or familiar spirits, are the manifestation of thought-forms that appear as an animal. The animal can be an actual animal, or it can come to you in a dream. The most important aspect of the familiar is that it is deliberately called into being by the practitioner. In times past, some witches were also believed to possess the skill of turning into animals themselves, either as a deception or as protection.

A familiar is a partner in magickal work from the natural world. The familiar serves as a conduit between human intellect and animal instinct. Animals possess many gifts of wisdom that we can learn from, the least of which is how to live in harmony with our environment. Working with familiars is advanced magick. Familiars may act as temple guardians and may choose to participate in rituals. It is not uncommon for a familiar to channel a mythological role. Paying attention to the behavior of animals and how they interact with humans within the context of magickal ritual can give the practitioner great insight into the intersections between the worlds.

49. **Turtle:** The turtle walks between the worlds of water and land. The turtle was believed to be the beginning of life on earth. Turtle Island was a mythical place in the center of the earth where a great waterland existed. The turtle emerged and brought with it the moral code by which we all must live.

50. **Weasel:** The weasel represents adjustment. Living in colonies, weasels are small but sacred. They stay close to the ground and use their gift of ingenuity to change their fur to mimic their surroundings. White weasels are called ermines.

51. **Whale:** The whale is the great historian. One of the most long-lived of all creatures, the whale is the ancient ancestor of the sea and the keeper of the wisdom of time.

52. **Wolf:** The wolf represents gratitude. Always working together, wolves live and travel in packs for protection and survival. Wolves bring wisdom of how to heal the physical body as well as the benefits of cooperation. For these abilities, they embody perpetual gratitude.

RITUAL: CREATING HARMONY WITH ALL BEINGS: ADVANCED CIRCLE CASTING

The realm of natural magick can greatly inform traditional elements of witchcraft. One of the most significant of these is the practice of casting a circle. Casting a circle is an integral part of the working of magick. It creates a psychic boundary, defines a physical space, and elicits a transfiguration that allows witches to walk between the worlds and experience divine communion within an ephemeral temple construct. Often, you can cast a circle by combining three distinct elements: speaking or chanting an incantation or invocation (such as calling the quarters and cardinal elements); physically indicating the boundaries of the circle; and using magickal tools such as an athalme, wand, sword, or staff to augment the power of the action and the words. Casting a circle is usually part of a larger ritual or sacred rite; it sets the stage upon which the practitioners and deities or forces of nature can interact. Expanding upon this important ritual component will allow you to experience the circle in a new way. Whether your practice is solitary or with a coven, deepening your understanding of circle casting will add significant energy to your greater rites.

1. Begin with a visualization of the circle. Most will see it on a horizontal plane, either on or slightly above the earth. Hold this vision in your mind and levitate the circle while projecting it outward so that its circumference expands. Within this expansion are all the creatures of earth. Accept them with perfect love and perfect trust and accept their wisdom and experience as valid, much like your own.

2. Now, within your envisioned circle, place another circle on the vertical orientation so that it intersects the horizontal plane. In front of you, you will see the place where the two circles cross. This pattern will repeat behind you as well. As you create this visualization in your mind, you may find it helpful to hold a crystal ball or other spherical tool. Also, the use of hand gestures and ritual tools can help with the actualization of the circle.

3. When your two expanded circles are conjoined at intersecting planes, face the east. You will see the outline of the levitating expanded circle on the horizontal plane. Raise your arm over your head and using a ritual tool (if necessary) begin at the zenith point where the two circles join and create a third circle on the vertical plane. Bring your arm slowly down in front of you to delineate the curve of what is now the framework of a sphere. You will now see a cross in front of you where the second vertical circle intersects with the horizontal plane.

4. Visualize the horizontal plane slowly lowering onto the ground so that you are standing under a dome of energy that includes all the creatures of the sky. The sphere continues underground, encompassing the burrowing creatures beneath the earth as well as the microscopic inhabitants of the soil. Within the protected sphere are the energetic reverberations of the denizens of earth and nature, including you. You exist at the center of this construct, able to invite specific energies inside in order to accomplish the task at hand.

The Modern Witchcraft Book of Natural Magick

5. You will find that the energy within the sphere will change according to the seasons. Encompassing all life-forms within the sacred circle will help you to attune to their unique rhythms and cycles. You will note when the cardinals appear, when the robins return, when the trees lie dormant, and when the branches bud out. Creating the circle, which is actually a sphere, in this manner, with precise and deliberate visualizations, also strengthens it. You will be far more hesitant to violate ritual protocols by allowing people to pass in and out without preparation and grounding if you have invested so much of your own energy in this creative endeavor.

6. A cast circle is much larger and more powerful than a circle drawn on the ground. It permeates the above and the below, a reflection of the beauty of the sublunary world and all the life energy that it contains. It should be dismantled with the same amount of care and attention with which it is built. As you become adept at the visualization, you may even be able to narrate the construct in real time in order to teach other practitioners about the scope and depth of the circle within whose borders they gather. When the circle is open, it remains unbroken, awaiting the call of the natural magick witch to bring it into being once again.

SPELL TO ATTUNE WITH NATURE: ABOVE AND BELOW THE CONE OF POWER

Raising a cone of power is a traditional ritual of witchcraft. This is often a part of coven work with a high priestess or facilitator directing the group energy as it builds to a climax, then directing the energy to the divine goddess in perfect trust that she will aid and further activate the intention for which the cone was raised.

It is important to note that each participant in natural magick has her own energy signature. Think of the way a pendulum gyrates. From each person attending the ritual, a cone is produced. The iconic conical hat with a wide brim that witches are frequently depicted as wearing is an excellent visual for this; however, it is far from complete.

Imagine the natural magick practitioner as the center point of her own personal circle of energy on the ground. Each witch is within her own circle. This circle extends upward to form a cone. It also encompasses all of nature that exists within that field of energy: the spirits of air, the winged creatures—insects and birds—as well as the creatures of the land. Additionally, another cone emanates from that same circle, only this one extends downward, into the earth, aligning the practitioner with the root energy of plants, the microscopic organisms of the soil, and the denizens of the subterranean world. When you raise a cone of power, either solitary or with a coven, you can access the intricacies of these energetic relationships through the cultivation of awareness.

Think about all the beings that your cone will encompass, and see yourself as a part of this complex web of nature. You may also draw energy up from the deep earth and conjure visions of harmony with the unseen world. Many things may be revealed to you as you deepen your experience within the cone of power. Although frequently used in coven craft, the cone of power is truly an individual construct. When you visualize yourself at the center of the cone that radiates in both directions, you begin to see yourself with greater clarity within the context of nature.

Even when coven members focus their energy into a cone produced by a group, they are all acting from within the sphere of their own individual energetic signatures. It is possible to transfer this energy into a collective cone if each participant is of a singular focus. If you are the high priestess of the coven, you can provide instruction on the specific visualization elements that are required of each coven member and gauge the effectiveness as you direct the central cone. Recognizing the place of each individual within the magickal network of esoteric energy will assist the coven and will deepen your practice. Do not be surprised if natural manifestations appear to you, such as a gathering wind, a clap of thunder, or the appearance of wild creatures or insects. A spider may descend on a silken thread in your midst, or you may hear the cry of a falcon overhead. Nature will frequently react and respond to witches who acknowledge and actively seek alignment and act in harmony with her vast power.

CHARM: CHARGING A CRYSTAL

Crystals are frequently used as ritual tools. Quartz, in particular, is an excellent conductor, and many witches use these minerals to amplify a spell, adapt them into a charm, or use them as part of a ritual tool. You will frequently see quartz crystals and other gems and minerals in wands and amulets, and they are used as ritual adornment. Because they are such efficient conductors of energy, there is sometimes a desire to cleanse or clear a crystal of any residual energy before dedicating it for magickal purposes. Some practitioners achieve this through connecting the mineral with the elements, either by burying it in the earth for a lunar cycle or exposing it to sunlight or moonbeams before using it for ritual purpose.

Once the crystal has been cleared, it is easy to charge it with your own energy. All you need to do is create a vibration. Hold the crystal in the palm of one hand and clap over it with the other hand. Another method is by striking the crystal against your altar or ritual tools with a light tapping motion. Crystals form in regular geometric patterns and have cleavage planes that are prone to breakage, so you do not want to strike them with excessive force.

Each mineral and element has its own specific electromagnetic charge. An inherent charge will not transfer; that is to say, you cannot lay a crystal on a sheet of copper and expect it to resonate with the same charge as copper. Striking the crystal with iron will not change its charge to that of iron. These same concepts that apply to the physical world also apply to the metaphysical world. Abstract concepts such as love, courage, or anger have their own charge and affect our physical bodies differently. We are physical incarnations of spiritual beings, so our experience is always filtered through the physical realm. Emotional states will affect how we experience our physical state. Similarly, a crystal will form under specific conditions and become a conduit for energy other than its own. By creating a vibration with sound or contact on your crystal, you can impart an energetic principle that will be conducted through the lattice.

You can test the effects of the charge with a pendulum, a balanced rod, or similar divining tool. You can expect to see a different reaction in the divining tool before and after charging. A dramatic way to experience this is by observing the results of divining once a chemical change has transpired. Take a match and hover over it with your divining tool until you get an observable reaction. Then, using tweezers, hold the match after you strike it, allowing it to burn down completely. Test the charred remains with the same divining tool. You will see a distinct difference in the energy signature of the wood after it has been reduced to carbon.

Familiarize yourself with the subtleties of divining, and soon you will not even need a tool for interpretation and detection of a change in energy. You will be able to synthesize the information you get from the physical world, however subtle it may be. Dedicate your crystal to its new purpose and allow its natural conductive properties to work in alignment with your will. We are all creatures of the earth, with a place among the beauty of the forests, the depths of the oceans, the flyways of migrating birds. When we approach the earth as an entity, we acknowledge our place along the glittering strands of the web of life. Whether we experience these as energetic emanations; the threads woven in a protective network across, over, and through our beloved planet with the ability to heal and regulate itself; or as physical places along the ley lines of a vast and untamed landscape, we are all bound to this place for which we have many names. Some call her goddess. Some call her home. Since the beginning of recorded history, she has been understood as a female deity, her strength and power a protective fortress for all her creatures. Explore her and care for her. Accept her gifts of wisdom as you interact with the singular most important experiential facet of natural magick. Gaia, the primordial mother, beckons you to answer her call. Her mysteries and magick await you. Become her steward, her champion as you learn to live in harmony with her power and might. Turn your eyes to the heavens, and there you will see her shining sister, reflecting the light of the sun back to you.

Chapter Eight

SILVER LEAF AND LUNAR TIDE

The Realm of the Moon

No other celestial body resonates with magick quite like the moon. Our nearest neighbor in the heavens, the moon has been associated with divinity since the dawn of recorded history. Powerful goddesses of civilizations past captivated the minds of her followers and inspired ritual, incantation, worship, and magick. Specific lunar phases were identified with certain aspects of the goddess. Lunar imagery has been associated with Isis, Hathor, and Astarte in the Egyptian pantheon. To the Phoenicians, she was Ashtoreth; in Babylonia she was worshipped as Ishtar, the Queen of Heaven. In Sumer, the Queen of Heaven and Earth was Inanna. In classical Greece, she was Artemis. The Romans knew her as Diana. Rays of moonlight were known as Artemis's arrows, and the children of Diana were believed to have been faeries born from moonlight. Artemis and Diana were huntresses, depicted with silver bows, both virginal and wild. Like Astarte, their association was with the crescent moon. Hecate, the ancient crone of wisdom, had her place low in the sky, associated with either the rising or setting moon when it appears largest to earthly observers. And Selene, who was often depicted driving a chariot of white horses across the sky, would watch over her beloved Endymion as he slept.

The moon governs the tides and affects all patterns of life. More babies are born within two days of the full moon than at any other time. Additionally, more babies are born at or just after high tide. Human beings have been documenting lunar activity as far back as 750 B.C.E. The oldest and most reliable astronomical observation was made by Babylonia astronomers who kept detailed records. It is likely that the recorded observation of the 721 B.C.E. lunar eclipse was significant in the eyes of the beholders. The fascination with the moon transcended earthly boundaries. It was the Greeks who discovered the moon's reflective nature and that at any given time, only half of it could be seen.

The moon is an object of never-ending transformation. As the moon changes its position in relation to the sun, we are able to observe its phases. The lunar cycle is also connected to a woman's menstrual cycle, as it takes twenty-eight and a quarter days for the moon to complete a phase of lunation cycles. Medieval herbalists were known to treasure moon lore. It was believed that flowering herbs planted under a full moon would yield twice as many blossoms as a plant sown under less auspicious circumstances.

MEDITATION: PHASES OF THE MOON: TO RISE, FIRST SHE MUST FALL

Each phase of the moon brings with it specific energies that can be focused on in order to attune with the laws of nature, the movement of heavenly bodies, and their effects upon the sublunary world. The moon affects not only the waters and the tides; it also has a significant pull on our minds. Darkness must be acknowledged and confronted, and the moon is our instrument of understanding. When the moon is dark, before the first sliver of crescent appears in the sky, we acknowledge the energy of chaos, the frenetic charge before order. In the new moon, we glimpse hidden changes, the things that otherwise remain unseen. This is the time of new beginnings. When darkness is integrated, there are lessons to be learned and insight to be gained. This is the time of fulfillment and activity. It is not a time of illumination, for the moon shows us only reflected light; it has no light source of its own. Even in darkness, beauty and wholeness, completion and fulfillment, are understood and experienced by the natural magick practitioner. The first quarter moon is the time of coming forth, of germination and beginnings. The second quarter represents the continuum of development. Here, actions have already been set into motion, and the time of waxing has begun. The third quarter is a time of maturity, of fullness and completion, while the fourth quarter is the time for rest and introspection, disintegration and the promise of once again beginning anew.

In this lunar goddess meditation, you will be asked to face your dark side without fear, but with acceptance and understanding. You will follow the descent of the powerful moon goddesses of Mesopotamia whose myths still resonate to this day. This exercise is designed to strip away the ego, to concede personal identity and break down defenses until only love remains. It is a powerful journey to be used during initiatory rites or during major life changes or upheavals.

- Imagine yourself in a state of power and protection. You are embarking on a journey to an unknown psychic realm. You are regal and radiant, adorned with all the glorious trappings of prestige and accomplishment. Upon your head is a silver crown set with stars. You wear this as a symbol of the sovereignty of the high priestess. In daily life, you take on many different roles and responsibilities, not all of which come with emblems of recognition, but here in the psychic realm, you are recognized as powerful, and your crown announces you as a woman of power.

- You wear impressive earrings. Not only are they beautiful, but they also allow you a certain portal to divine intuition. You are gifted with the power of hearing beyond the natural world, able to glean messages and understanding from the unseen world. Around your neck is an amulet that radiates warmth. The love of your heart imbues this amulet, and you wear it proudly as an enduring symbol of your connection to the life-giving power of love. Upon each wrist, you wear a wide cuff bracelet. These are imbued with magick, allowing you to bend the forces of nature for the good of all beings. Around your waist is a jeweled girdle, a wide belt embroidered with metallic threads of silver and gold and set about with glittering gemstones of every color. You wear anklets with wings; their appearance is in alignment with their enchantment. Your winged feet allow you to move effortlessly according to your will. Finally, concealing your great beauty is a gossamer veil of unequaled power. This veil protects you and shields you so that you may walk between the worlds and return unharmed.

- On your journey, you come to a crossroads. You take the western path, and soon you come to a forbidding gate. Beyond the gate lies your desire, your reason for setting out on this journey. An insurmountable barrier has manifested between you and your greatest desire. Full of confidence and power, you knock on the gate until it trembles. You feel as though you could smash through it if you had to, but just as this feeling rises, a guardian appears. He allows you passage through the gate, but only if you surrender your crown.

- You think of all the times you have gone unrecognized, the sacrifices you have made, the times you were overlooked or ignored, and you hesitate. Relinquishing your crown means giving up the emblem of your achievements, so hard-won and so rarely acknowledged. It is difficult, but you must continue. You remove your crown from beneath your veil and lay the sparkling object at the feet of the gatekeeper.
- The doors swing open and you continue your descent. The road slopes downward, a declining plane into darkness. You notice a drop in temperature as you come to a second gate. Here you encounter another guardian who requires your earrings in exchange for passage. You pause. Your earrings give you the ability to hear beyond the mundane world. They are your link to your intuition. Understanding that your journey is more important than any personal effects, you slowly remove your earrings and offer them to the guardian of the gate. As soon as you do, the gates swing open, and you continue downward.
- Feeling somewhat ordinary and slightly dull, you take cautious steps forward and confront the third gate. The gatekeeper stops you and requires that you surrender your necklace. Your hands fly to your heart, protecting it. Hesitating, you feel the amulet pulsing with life, attuned to your own heartbeat. To remove it feels as if you are giving up the very warmth of your own heart. With a deep sigh, you unclasp the necklace and hand it to the guardian. Again, the mighty doors of the forbidding gate swing open.
- You are beginning to feel sorrowful and lost. With shaking steps you venture forward and find your journey impeded yet again. Another gate rises from the gathering darkness, the guardian of the gate barring you from proceeding unless you remove your

bracelets. You cross your hands over your heart. Your bracelets contain powerful magic. To give them up is to become completely ordinary. Comforted by the fact that you still have your emblems of strength and protection, you slip the bracelets off of your wrists and listlessly drop them before the gatekeeper. As if engaged by an unseen key, the gates respond to your acquiescence, and you are permitted passage.

- Cold begins to bite your skin, and you wrap your arms around yourself as you determinedly step forward into what feels like a widening abyss. Looming in the darkness is another mysterious gate with a guardian blocking your way. In exchange for passage, he requires the jeweled girdle that encircles your waist. You are shivering and exhausted, and your strength is already leaving you. Weariness is setting in. So much has been demanded of you already; surely you must continue down this dark and mysterious path. You surrender your girdle, and with a terrifying groan, the gates allow you to silently pass through.

- Deeper into the dampness and blackness you wander, sliding your feet forward with hesitant steps until your toe hits something hard and cold. Barely able to see or hear, you push your foot forward again, as if you could nudge this obstacle from your path. It is immovable, and you can go no farther. Out of the darkness, the gatekeeper appears and offers you passage in exchange for your anklets. You pause, for without your winged feet, how will you return to the upper realms from which you descended? Remembering that you are still protected by your veil, you trust that no harm will come to you, and you crouch down to unclasp your anklets. Like tinkling bells, they make a musical sound as they drop upon the cold, wet stones beneath your feet. You hear the groan of the gate opening, and you slowly walk through into darkness.

- Your path takes a sudden drop. You feel as if you are being pulled down, and you shift your body, practically leaning backward as you proceed in the effort to remain upright. The path is slippery, and the decline is steep. You feel that you are on the verge of losing your balance and sliding into an abyss until you hit the seventh and final gate. Frustrated, you knock haphazardly, calling for the guardian in a broken voice. A figure emerges from the shadows. You cannot see who it is, but you demand passage in a shaking and thin voice. Your passage is granted in exchange for your veil. Angry and exasperated, you rip off your veil and throw it at the shadow. You have now given up everything. Every bit of magic, everything that set you apart and made you special is gone. You have nothing left. You are hurt, tired, and drained and bereft of any raiment or finery. You are alone and unremarkable. Suddenly, the gates swing open, and you feel yourself tumbling down, falling into darkness, unable to grasp anything until you land with a thud, deep within the void. You struggle to get to your feet. You cannot rise. You strain your eyes to see. There is nothing but the void. You cry out, and your voice is silenced. You writhe through the mud, trying to grasp on to something, a memory, anything. Like fleeting moonbeams obscured by dark clouds, your memories fog over and fade. You do not even know who you are or why you came this way in the first place. Abject and forsaken, you start to become one with the void. There is nothing but absence, and you surrender yourself to it.

- At the moment of your surrender you have the growing feeling that you are not alone. While you can barely acknowledge the existence of yourself, still you know that someone is here with you. A tingling warmth begins to creep into your core. It spreads outward to your extremities, animating every cell in your body. You experience it as a radiant balm, as if rivers of gold were flowing through your veins. You breathe it in, and it sends ripples of pleasure through your body. You may not know who you are, but you instantly recognize the unmistakable power and presence of love. Filled with a sense of comforting peace and tranquil joy, you shudder with delight, happy in your minimal existence, happy to be free of everything except this permeating pleasure. You feel as if you could stay here forever. The love encompasses the whole of your being, and you bless it. In a whisper, you speak your blessing aloud.

- The moment that you do this, your eyes engage, and even in the pitch blackness you are able to see perfectly. For each black, there is a deeper black, and the shapes and silhouettes of your surroundings manifest in sharp and unmistakable focus. Right beside you is your own true love, the reason you allowed yourself to become so defenseless. Before you is a dark and towering throne, shining like obsidian. Seated on the throne is the Queen of the Dead. You recognize her immediately. She is your sister. Ereshkigal. Persephone. Morrigan. You know her well. And perhaps for the first time, you face her fearlessly. She seems surprised, possibly even shocked. Her voice resonating through your body, you feel her speak these words:

> *"Sister, indeed you have conquered death. You allowed*
> *yourself to become abject and unknown. You have sacrificed every*
> *part of yourself, and still you have blessed me and thanked me.*
> *You descended to my realm and met my terms, surrendering all your*
> *magic and power, all your finery and attributes. You wallowed in mud,*
> *not even remembering your divine nature. And you truly learned that I*
> *am nothing to fear. You approached me with nothing but love,*
> *and this love I now return to you."*

- Suddenly, like an ocean wave crashing over you, you remember everything. You know exactly who you are and everything of which you are capable. You take your true love by the hand, and together you rise. Your strength returns, and you begin your ascent together. Your trappings of grandeur are returned to you, and you triumphantly emerge into the shimmering moonlight together, completely restored and free.

RITUAL MAGICKA LUNA: DRAWING DOWN THE MOON

In the nineteenth-century book *Aradia: Gospel of the Witches*, the ritual of drawing down the moon is described. This sacred rite has remained popular and has its roots in natural magick, as it is best performed out of doors. It was considered common practice for mid-twentieth century witches to enact their rituals while skyclad. This practice also characterized modern magick as a bit scandalous. Combining the occult with the sensual was in alignment with the zeitgeist of the mid-twentieth century counterculture. Occult themes were interwoven in popular music, and there was renewed interest in occult societies. A major revival of witchcraft came about during this time, and the echoes of it are still resonating today.

In drawing down the moon, the priestess or witch becomes the embodiment of the lunar goddess. This practice is believed to have originated in ancient Greece, performed by the Thessalian witches who captured the imagination of many, including Lucius Apuleius, who wrote of their sorcery, enchantment, and mystery with an almost obsessive air. Thessaly cultivated an aura of magick that persisted for centuries and is believed to have had a significant impact on modern practice. Aradia was the daughter of Diana and is understood to be the first witch who taught the ritual of drawing down to the witches of earth. The ritual is best performed out of doors. Enacting the rite skyclad is a personal decision and not a requirement. Being skyclad is meant to represent freedom and autonomy. What follows is an adaptation of this centuries-old ritual.

You will need:

- A glass bowl
- Spring water
- A mirror
- An invocation of your own creation
- A chant to honor the Moon Goddess
- Scrying
- A libation
- Crescent-shaped cakes, baked and consecrated by you or another coven member
- An offering of thanks

Directions:

1. Pour the water into the bowl and using the mirror, reflect the light of the moon into the bowl. Invoke the goddess of the moon,

choosing the aspect with which you most highly resonate and have the most scholarly knowledge or personal gnosis. Channel your own invocation extemporaneously or have one prepared in advance. Make your intention clear. You will need to craft the invocation with strong intention. Required in the invocation are the request for divine presence and the bestowal of wisdom from the deity to the witch or priestess.

2. Using the water in the bowl, scry and keep a watchful observance of natural manifestations such as the presence of animals or interactions of nature, including a gathering wind or some other such sign. When the manifestation is acknowledged and the divine presence is felt, pour a libation into the earth. This can be spring water or wine, representing a return to origin and communion with the goddess. Consume a portion of it, establishing the link between the moon, the witch, and the land. Then, eat the consecrated cakes and scatter the crumbs as an offering of thanks.

Consecrated Crescent Cakes

This recipe for consecrated crescent cakes is a powerful spell. It requires significant energy, a commitment to process, and a willingness of the practitioner to forgo certain conveniences in order to imbue the cakes with an energetic signature. These cakes will complement the ritual of drawing down the moon.

SERVES THIRTEEN
- 16 ounces of heavy cream
- 2½ cups of unbleached all-purpose flour
- 1 tablespoon of baking powder
- ¼ teaspoon of baking soda
- A dash of salt
- 4 tablespoons of honey, divided evenly

1. Pour the heavy cream into a clean quart jar with a tight-fitting lid. Seal the jar.
2. Vigorously shake the jar for 30–35 minutes. As you vigorously shake the jar, allow yourself to enter into a meditative state.

3. Set a steady rhythm to the shaking and align it with your breath. When you get into a flow, use a goddess chant to help you stay focused:

"Isis, Astarte, Diana, Hecate, Demeter, Kali, Inanna!"

4. After 30–35 minutes of vigorous shaking, the cream will separate into buttermilk and butter. Pour off the liquid into a 1 cup measure. Use a spatula to press the butter to the sides of the jar to extract the most buttermilk. Set the buttermilk and butter aside.
5. Preheat the oven to 425°F.
6. Measure 2 tablespoons of the butter into a small glass bowl and set it on top of the warming oven to melt.
7. In a large bowl, combine the dry ingredients and stir them together rhythmically in a sunwise circle.
8. Add 5–6 tablespoons of your freshly made butter.
9. Using 2 knives, one in each hand, move your hands in opposite directions to blend the butter with the dry ingredients. Rotate the bowl periodically. Meditate on the four directions and the cardinal elements as you do this. The mixture will resemble fine crumbs.
10. Stir in two tablespoons of honey with a wooden spoon.
11. Add the buttermilk and stir energetically, scraping the bottom of the bowl periodically.
12. The dough will be sticky. Gradually add the remaining ½ cup of flour until the dough leaves the sides of the bowl.
13. Turn the dough out onto a lightly floured surface and knead. As you knead the dough, think of your reasons for enacting the drawing down the moon ritual and whisper them into the dough. Articulate what you hope to accomplish, insights you wish to gain, or blessing you hope to receive.
14. Press the dough flat with your hands to make it ½" high.
15. Lightly dust with flour a cup approximately 2½" diameter (or use a cookie cutter or biscuit cutter) and cut 4 (or 5 if you can fit it) circles out of the dough.

16. Position the cup ⅓ of the way in from the edge of each circle and press again to make the crescent shape.
17. Gather up the scraps and knead them together.
18. Press the remaining dough to ½" thick and repeat the process for cutting the crescents.
19. Transfer the crescents to a baking sheet lined with parchment paper. They should be placed about 1" apart.
20. In the small glass bowl, combine the remaining 2 tablespoons of honey with the melted butter and stir together to blend thoroughly.
21. Using a small pastry brush, brush the tops of the crescent cakes with the butter and honey mixture.
22. Slide the baking sheet into the oven as you say this spell:

"By my hand a mix is made. By fire it is forever changed. Through this transformation of light and heat, the spell is bound and the work is complete. May it be pleasing to all who are called to partake of the magick and nourishment of my crescent cake. So mote it be."

23. Bake for 10 minutes or until golden, usually no more than 13 minutes.
24. Remove the crescent cakes from the oven and brush them again with the remaining butter and honey mixture.
25. Share with your ritual companions.

The many steps involved in making these crescent cakes are important for the natural magick practitioner to experience. Yes, you could go out and purchase buttermilk and butter for the sake of convenience, but starting from scratch gives you a stronger connection to the spell. Remember, you are not just creating a snack; you are creating a magickal offering, and the more energy you put into it, the more you will get out of it. Take each step seriously as a way to interact with the natural world and put forth the time and effort to reap the benefits of the sacred work. The work is joyful. Sing and chant and move about as you create!

SPELL: CLAIRVOYANCE AND THE MAGICK MIRROR

The art of scrying under the full moon is done to increase psychic abilities. Most practitioners of natural magick experience some form of psychic awareness in varying degrees. Like any other skill, cultivation and practice lead to an increase of abilities, particularly if you have a natural aptitude. Often, a level of psychic awareness manifests as a physical sensation, such as a tingling of the crown chakra. Other times, it can manifest as intuition, a subtle but firm "knowing" regarding details of a specific situation that has not been explicitly revealed.

The moon acts as an amplifier to the innate talent of the witch who seeks to develop her gifts. Additionally, there are tools of the craft that can be created to facilitate this process. Having the correct ritual tool is important, as it can impact the results.

1. To create a magick mirror for developing clairvoyance, you will need a round glass like those found in picture frames or from the face of a clock. You can find such items at flea markets or antique shops. On the night of the new moon, paint the convex side with a coat of black enamel. As the moon waxes, continue adding a layer each night until you have achieved an opaque surface. Allow it to dry thoroughly. When you have achieved sufficient coverage, the glass will become a reflective mirror.

2. Wait until the moon is full and then expose the glass to moonlight for as long as you are able. Afterward, wrap the glass in a dark, opaque cloth and keep it carefully stored, taking extra precaution never to expose it to sunlight. It is important that the mirror is never used for anything other than magick and that it is properly charged under the full moon a few times a year or before you intend to use it.

3. To scry with your magick mirror, place it before you on your altar. You can also make a stand for it or otherwise prop it up so that you can gaze into it comfortably. Use a white candle to illuminate your face and make sure this light is not directed at the mirror. Begin with an intention of what you hope to see. This may be something from the past, such as a past life, or something from the future, such as something that is about to come into being. Whatever

your intention, focus on the mirror and relax and open your mind to the images that come to you. Do not attempt to censor or interpret the images. Just let them flow. After your scrying session, you can record your sensations, whether they are physical or intuitive, and look for symbolism and patterns. Take notes of your insights so that you are able to track your progress.

Other tools used for scrying are crystal balls, bowls of water, and even the reflection of the moon itself on the waves of the sea. However you intend to engage the moon, remember that it is by nature changing and reflective. Revelations will come in the subtlest of forms. Attune your senses to interpret things that may otherwise go easily overlooked. This is the power of Magicka Luna.

CHARM: ARTEMISIA, THE SILVER LEAF

A lunar charm can augment the energy of the moon, allowing you an extra surge when you have need of it. The moon is mysterious and often associated with chaos and uncertainty. Creating a charm can provide a sense of grounding during turbulent times. State your purpose in creating your charm by the light of the moon. Some suggestions are:

- An aid to divination that mysteries may be revealed to the wearer or holder of the charm.
- An answer to a question that will become manifest while the charm is active.
- Clarity and insight into a confusing situation.

Once you have determined your purpose, gather your materials.

You will need:

- White candles
- A cup of water
- Stick of incense
- A smooth, tumbled moonstone

- A polished silver coin or tiny mirror
- Artemisia or mugwort leaf, freshly gathered
- A silver thread embroidery floss to bind the charm

Directions:

1. Work by the light of the moon, or if you are practicing indoors, at your altar alight with white candles. Let there be a cup of water and a stick of incense to represent the other elements. If you are practicing out of doors, you will not need these things. You will be surrounded by the elements and will feel their presence without the need of tools.

2. Place the moonstone on top of the coin or mirror. Wrap the artemisia leaf around them with the silver side facing out and begin binding them together with the embroidery floss, holding a "tail," about a foot long, hanging free (for tying off at the end). Wind the thread around carefully, laying each thread beside the other, crossing over the center point, and moving around the circle so a weblike pattern begins to appear. As you wind the thread, speak your intent and purpose.

3. When you are satisfied, cut the thread, leaving a length of one foot. Bring the two long ends together and loop them around your finger. Feed the two ends through the loop, leaving the loop open. Put a needle through the open loop and use the needle to slide a knot down to the edge of the wrapped bundle. Remove the needle and tie off the ends. You can wear the charm around your neck, keep in it your pocket, or keep it on your altar. By the time the leaves are dry, the efficacy of the charm will manifest.

The phases of the moon beckon witches to gather. Full moons and new moons mark the passage of time outside of the Gregorian calendar. Following the cycles of lunation, becoming familiar with tidal patterns, and observing the rise and fall are ways to align your natural magick practice with lunar energy. All life on earth is dependent upon water, and all water is pulled by the gravitational force of the moon. The moon holds sway over our moods and our minds. If ever you have danced by the light of the moon and seen your own shadow fall across the land long after the sun has departed the sky, then you know how it feels to be attuned to the living goddess when magick is afoot. The lunation cycle is our best representation of the triple goddess; in the phases of the moon we see the maiden, mother, and crone. We are constantly reminded that the one and only constant is change, and that change is the very essence of magick.

Chapter Nine

STAR MAGICK

The Realm of Cosmos

O n a moonless summer night, it is possible to see the glittering spiral arm of the Milky Way galaxy stretch across the black velvet sky.

We see the beauty and intricacy of this dancing spiral glittering in the stars above and in the patterns of nature below; the spiral pattern manifests in the seed bearers of coniferous trees, in the architecture of the shell of the chambered nautilus, and in the succulent plants of the desert. Our tiny solar system, hardly remarkable against the multitude of star systems that inhabit our beautiful spiraling pocket of the universe, has been perfectly positioned to support our individual and unique requirement for life. We are famously made of stardust. Our connection to the cosmic realm is constantly echoed in the natural patterns of our earthbound world. We need only look to gain awareness of our connection to the greater reality and fully realize that as it is above, so also it is below.

The foundation of modern cosmology depends on our conditioned view of the world: the entirety of the all-encompassing universe, including each of us as individuals as well as our observations about what we perceive. The popular cosmogony, or creation myth, prevalent today is the big bang theory, a creation concept with a peculiar void of creativity. It contains no implicit traditions but instead is centered on an incredibly unlikely series of atomic and subatomic reactions disconnected from any sense of custom. It is an egocentric product of an imposing masculine mind.

Creation is reflexive. Reality tends to shape itself and respond to however we are conditioned or taught to imagine it. According to Hans-Peter Dürr, a former professor of quantum physics and director of the Max Planck Institute for Physics in Munich, Germany, "Creation is not finished. The world occurs anew every moment." The famed Greek philosopher Socrates, who is known as the father of modern thought, postulated that there is a "pattern in the heavens which anyone can find and establish within themselves." Everything is woven together in a sacred fabric that we may access at any time.

As practitioners of natural magick, we know this fabric makes up a core element of ritual. Restorative choices made in the spirit of individual agency reverberate outwardly and touch the far corners of the universe. Deity manifests to the devotee as a revealer of order and truth. Cosmic systems have the ability to instill a sense of societal harmony. Especially in coven craft, when you have the direct experience that your work is much larger than you are as an individual, that the participation and presence of others acts as an energetic amplifier, you may send a cone of power into the greater universe with the full confidence that it will be guided to its mark. Goddess energy radiates from a central point. Even our traditional units of measure, such as feet for distance or length and pounds for weight, are based on celestial proportions. Perhaps it is for this reason that these arcane quantifiers have proven so difficult to replace. We are hesitant to discard our connections to divine proportion.

MEDITATION: THE COSMOGONY OF BRINGING CHAOS TO ORDER: CREATIVITY AND CREATION

Our connection to the sacred is not involuntary. It must be cultivated. So much of the alienation prevalent in society today can be attributed to our unconscious abandonment of this connection, this loss of understanding when it comes to proportion and the repeating patterns of nature. There is a divine proportion and order from which we can benefit immensely if we only open our minds to its observation.

"You do not have to be a New Ager to conclude that the only world order in which human nature can happily exist is the sacred order, the cosmological expression of ideal harmony and proportion which constituted the esoteric base behind every ancient lasting civilization."
—John Michell, author of How the World Is Made:
The Story of Creation According to Sacred Geometry

We can just as easily attract happiness and good fortune if we make it a practice to attune our minds to do so. Too often, we unconsciously attune our natural gifts to things we do not even want! Shallow ideas, gossip, and negative energy creep in only due to their prevalence and our lack of intentional cultivation of other, more beneficial thought-forms to take their place. This meditation should become part of your natural magick practice as a way to engage with harmonious energy that otherwise remains unseen and unexperienced. There are creative benefits to exploring the patterns of ratio and proportion. Patterns perfect and divine are all around you. You will be surprised how these invisible entities interact with your own field of influence immediately upon your awareness.

- Begin by detaching from technology, electricity, and any and all artificial stimulation. Envelop yourself in darkness. Close your eyes and call to yourself a vision. It fills your mind's eye with a kind of static. It is as if you are gazing up at the velvet blackness of the night sky, strewn with stars, but the stars are far more numerous and contain an exciting and observable energy. If you can envision a television set without reception or the chaotic movement of microwave rays, this is the image that you must hold in your mind. It is silver, gray, and the deepest black, flecks of light furiously interacting with each other, attracting and repelling without any discernable rhyme or reason. The sound you hear could be the buzz of bees, the hum of scurrying flies, crumpling paper, a downpour of rain, or a sizzling skillet all sounding at once. The noise matches the static, chaotic and unrehearsed. You allow yourself to experience this primordial chaos as a part of its dimension. Light and sound, depth and movement, darkness and disorder are all present before you.
- Then, from beyond the veil of nature, a silver thread emerges. The creatrix sets the thread into motion, and it begins to spin. It spins itself into a sphere; however, it is far from inanimate. It is a living creature, spherically shaped, fashioned by an unseen hand into the most perfect of shapes containing a body, a soul, and a spirit. The chaos you have so carefully pictured begins to bring itself to order,

coalescing into a perfect, shimmering, silver sphere. It is as if all the random patterns of energy have drawn themselves toward each other. You are witnessing this attraction; in fact, it exists and comes into being specifically because of you, the observer.

- The sphere moves within itself, emanating from a central point with no discernable dimension. This cosmic center is shrouded in mystery. While you find it difficult to describe, you are nonetheless able to interact with it. Within this sphere, this perfection of shape, you experience creation as the generation of simple relationships and simple shapes. Within the sphere, you begin to see another sphere. This is the spherical formation of the earth within the orbit of the moon. You are creating a vision of the sublunary world.

- Out of the primordial chaos, the harmony of two interacting spheres takes form. You observe their proportional ratio, their relative distance from one another. In between these two, another simple shape begins to materialize. It is a square that frames the inner sphere and connects it with the outer sphere. While the silhouettes of circles have no ending and no beginning, the square is more finite. The divine eternal element of creation connects to solid matter, the plane of the earth. This square, this table is representative of human works. The square is the table of your altar. It is the magickal place where the dome of heaven touches the earth. The earth is divided from the heavens as represented by the circle in the square. Even though they are separate, they intersect and are connected to each other.

- Within the squared spheres, you begin to see more shapes materialize. These are equilateral triangles, interlocked, with one pointing upward and one pointing down. These represent the land separated from the ocean. Your plane of reality is taking shape, but you are able to observe it in its purest form: simple shapes, perfectly proportioned, nesting within each other as though it were purposefully created in the form of geometric harmony. You are observing the transcendental interaction of the earth and the moon, the sky with the earth, the land with the sea. Within the heavenly circle and the earthly square are the generative powers of the sun as well as the reflective powers of the moon. You begin to see vivid colors as the black void of space separates into spectral colors when the light of stars passes through the geometric planes.

RITUAL CELESTIA: INVOCATION TO THE SEVEN SISTERS

In natural magick, to invoke the ethereal beings of the stellar sphere is to place one's self within the swirling cosmos and acknowledge that although we are small in relation to the vast expanse of the universe, we are no less significant. The candles that we light to invoke the goddess have the same power as the vestal flames ignited in temples of old. By calling to ourselves the energy of powerful deities, we establish a link between ourselves as individual practitioners and the fabric of the universe, the canopy of stars, and our remote temple, altar, or physical being. We become part of the cosmic web, able to receive messages in the form of oracles and manifestations.

1. Let your altar be draped with a black cloth to represent the night sky. In the west, place a chalice of milk; almond, soy, or dairy will suffice as it is the color that is most important. You may also sweeten it with honey. On the center of your altar, place seven tapered candles upright in holders in a circle. In each quadrant, you may set your ritual tools in their corresponding elemental quadrant and purify the space as well as yourself, then call the directions and elements. Begin with an invocation to the goddess:

   "Dark mother in whom all secrets of the universe are contained, I ask for your divine presence. The unknowable realms of deep space are beyond my understanding. To you, these far corners of the universe are your cauldrons of creation. Out of the blackness of the void, we see the creation of galaxies, the birth of nebulas, the implosion of stars

whose light travels across unfathomable expanses to still reach our
eyes. I search you out, to enact in harmony a rite to honor you, your
daughters, your timeless nature, your mystery and power. Be here now!"

2. If you have preserved a fire from previous ritual, you may use it
   to light the candles; otherwise, striking a match is the preferred
   method because it creates a physical interaction between the practitioner and the flame. Light the candles one by one, and with each
   lighting, make an incantation. If practicing with a coven, each
   member can take on a different incantation:

   "Alcyone of the silver flame, reach through the depths of eternity
   to bring us your spiritual light."

   "Maia, thou who art the mother of Hermes, bring us your message
   of clarity that we may see truth and balance love with wisdom."

   "Taygete, bringer of joy, we ask for the sweetness of your harvest of
   honey to touch our souls that sadness may depart and happiness reign."

   "Electra, the dark one, from beyond the shadowy veil your beauty shines
   forth. Bless us with your gift of loyalty, ever bright."

   "Sterope, twin star, we invoke your gift of friendship.
   May we know companionship and understanding; may we
   gather in your honor to celebrate these bonds."

   "Celaeno, star mother, connect us one to the other as your
   daughters. Bind us with your silvery thread that we may transcend
   this earthly sphere and know the eternal nature of our souls."

   "Merope, the unseen, grant us acceptance of the unknowable. Mysterious
   star, occulted star, your presence is deeply felt though you
   are beyond the reach of our eye. May fearlessness be ours."

3. Take the chalice and hold it aloft while you speak these words:

*"In the name of the white moon among the stars, I call upon
the goddess to descend into our sacred space. May we be blessed by
her divine presence. She who sets the stars in motion, from whose body
flows forth the rivers of celestial beings, bring us your far-reaching
light that we may shine forth your beauty, power, and wholeness of
being. May we become the protectors of all beings, for we are all born
of stars. In our bodies, we are linked to the heavens. May this bond
be strengthened. May we know health, vitality, and peace. May we
be in harmony with divine will and all the unseen energies of the
cosmos known and unknown. So mote it be."*

4. Drink the contents of the chalice and take a few moments to contemplate the altar ablaze with starlight. Use this space for meditation or for sharing experiences. Energy may be raised by whispering the names of the Seven Sisters, growing progressively louder as the dynamic surges. The vocalizations may transform into a mantra or primordial sound, reach an apex, and then subside. In the following calm, offer thanks:

*"For millennia, we have gazed at the Pleiades in wonder.
Many visions have been granted. We have seen the maidens' escape
from the hunter, a cluster of happy children dancing together, a reward
for victory, the flight of doves, and the gentle rain. Daughters of
Pleione and companions to Artemis, we give thanks for your
presence and your wonders, seen and unseen."*

5. If you are performing the ritual out of doors under the night sky, you will be able to locate the Pleiades overhead. From early fall and throughout the winter, the Pleiades appear just after sunset. In summer, they appear in the middle of the night. Find the three stars that comprise the belt of Orion. They will point to the constellation Taurus, which contains the bright star Aldebaran. Follow the line from Orion to Taurus and you will find the Pleiades.

After contemplation, you may release the star maidens as you extinguish the candles. Perform a grounding exercise before opening the circle and releasing the directions.

MUSICA UNIVERSALIS: THE MUSIC OF THE SPHERES

In music, two of the most pleasing intervals to any ear are what are known as the perfect fourth and the perfect fifth. Members of the classical Greece Pythagorean cult hypothesized that the ratio between intervals on the musical scale mirrored the relative distance between celestial bodies in our solar system. Music follows a geometric pattern, much like everything else in the universe. When you explore these intervals and ratios, you bring sound into your magic.

1. While adding bells, chimes, rainsticks, drums, sistrums, and strings can greatly enhance your natural magick practice, you do not need to be a musician or rhythmist to experience the music of the spheres. All you need are eight glasses of water, filled to different capacities. Pour an inch of water into one glass, into the next, two inches of water, three inches in the next, and so forth until the eighth, for which you may need to substitute a vase or a carafe. With a spoon, gently strike the side of the first glass to produce a tone. Then, strike the glass with four inches of water. Look at the distance in between their respective water levels. Listen for the harmonic balance between the tones. Repeat the listening exercise by striking the first glass again and then the one with five inches of water.

2. Allow the sound to drift through your mind as you explore the ratios of sound and distance in your thoughts. Visualize the space between the first and the fourth, as well as the first and the fifth. Make a pattern by lightly chiming one, four, one, then one, five, one. Create different patterns against a slow and steady rhythm. Add in some of the other notes for variety. See how the relative distances impact the melodic harmony. Are there intervals that create dissonance in your mind? How do you experience the relationship between the fourth and the fifth?

Ancient astronomers believed the secrets to the universe could be heard through the music of the spheres. These patterns were the same ratios that life on earth follows. The great philosopher Plato believed that the heavens could be divided along the paths of the revolving planets, and that each one made a sound as it traveled through space. Perhaps, he and others speculated, the same sound would be mirrored in the musical scale by the note that occupied the same relative distance and ratio on the scale. The astronomer Johannes Kepler believed that there was an inherent harmony in the celestial sphere.

CHARM: COSMIC CORRESPONDENCES TO EARTHBOUND ELEMENTS

Creating a charm creates a bond between the physical world and the psychic plane. A charm can be used to augment a spell or in place of a spell. Understanding correspondences can assist the efficacy of charms and spells. This reference chart is intended to allow the natural magick practitioner to choose appropriate energies to create effective charms.

PLANETARY CORRESPONDENCES				
Planet	*Shape*	*Color*	*Stone*	*Plant*
Moon	Crescent	Silver	Moonstone or pearl	Jasmine
Mercury	Septagon	Light blue	Opal or beryl	*Styrax*
Venus	Hexagon	Green	Emerald or peridot	Rose
Earth	Square	All colors	Agate	Dittany of Crete
Mars	Pentagon	Red	Garnet	Tobacco
Jupiter	Triangle	Royal blue	Amethyst	Cedar
Saturn	Octagon	Black	Onyx	Myrrh
Sun	Circle	Yellow	Amber or citrine	Frankincense

ZODIAC CORRESPONDENCES TO ELEMENTS			
Air	*Fire*	*Water*	*Earth*
Gemini	Leo	Cancer	Taurus
Libra	Sagittarius	Pisces	Virgo
Aquarius	Aries	Scorpio	Capricorn

The earliest priests were astronomers. For millennia, we have looked to the celestial sphere for influences upon our daily lives. Integrating star magick into your practice is a way to acknowledge your place in the vast expanse of the universe. There is beauty and order all around us. Divine proportion exists in the distance between the sun and the moon just as it does in our hands and feet. As we travel through space and time, we embrace our moment. Without the constant and deliberate movement of the planet around the sun, our concept of time would not exist. We measure our span in solar revolutions, with each return to our starting position a cause for celebration. Without the stars as a guide, exploration and navigation would surely have stalled. May we always look to the stars to understand our place in time. There is always time for magick.

The Modern Witchcraft Book of Natural Magick

Chapter Ten

NATURAL MAGICK FROM THE ANCIENTS

The Realm of Time

O ur concept of time owes itself to the revolution of the earth around the sun and the rotation of the earth on its axis. Outside of our plane of reality, time seems like an arbitrary construct, a unit of measure to help us understand the natural world. We reflect upon it, its ephemeral nature, and ponder how a simple measure of the passage of time in which the whole of our earthly lives is contained appears insignificant when measured against the distance of stars, the fossil record, or the whole of recorded history. Human lives are short, and the transfer of magickal knowledge has often been anecdotal. The earliest botanicals were intended to show the efficacy of medicinal and magickal uses of plants and herbs. Magick was inextricably linked with medicine, and some plants of legend were considered magickally potent.

The oldest herbal known is *Historia Plantarum*, or *History of Plants*, by Theophrastus. Compiled about 285 B.C.E., this work was significant in that it established a naturalistic basis for the science of botany. Subsequent compendiums kept the Theophrastean tradition alive and set the stage for the next phase of pharmacological and biological theory. There were practical applications to both agriculture and therapeutics. Pliny the Elder used Theophrastus's work in his seminal compendium, *Historia Naturalis*, which is regarded as the most significant compilation of all known natural history of its time. Pliny's book was the primary source of botanical information during the Middle Ages, and here is where things get really interesting. Medieval herbalists frequently referenced classical texts, but it was impossible for them to have any empirical knowledge of many of the herbs about which they spoke and wrote. Plant species specific to the Mediterranean basin, the Near East, and the Sahara could only be understood through the writings in earlier compendiums, not through direct observation. Descriptions of mythical plants are mingled in with real plants.

Herbal medicine was of vast importance during this time because in many cases it was the only available form of medical care. Wondrous healing powers as well as magickal effects were attributed to plants during the Middle Ages. There is a strong connection between magickal arts and plants used for therapeutic and medicinal purposes. Many of the desirable properties of certain plants were believed to be invoked by human action. Wellness and spirituality were closely linked.

Early herbal compendiums such as the Discorides herbal contain detailed descriptions along with illustrations of auspicious herbs and plants. Two important distinctions are made between potent herbs in early herbals; they are the magiferous plants and *plantae magicae*. Magiferous plants are different from *plantae magicae* in that the latter did not exist in nature. Often, they were connected to the invocation of romance, used for conjuring love, and were regarded as immanent but not of this earth; therefore, they did not follow the rules of nature. They were believed to have miraculous healing ability and did bear some connection to actual plants.

Magiferous plants, on the other hand, were real. These magick-bearing plants had their potency conferred upon them by acts of magick. Magiferous plants could acquire specific properties only when certain conditions were met. The magickal properties were not necessarily inherent to the plant, nor were they permanent. Magiferous plants include:

- Betony (*Stachys officinalis*)
- Celandine (*Chelidonium majus*)
- Mugwort (*Artemisia vulgaris*)
- Peony (*Paeonia*)
- Pervinca (*Vinca*)
- Rue (*Ruta graveolens*)
- Verbena (*Verbena officinalis*)

Magiferous plants came to be because there was a dearth of reliable medical care. Appealing to entities beyond the physical world enhanced the function of herbs and plants. The classical Greco-Roman traditions were preserved by the monastic orders for reasons that were practical, and while the *via antiqua* (or "old ways") continued to exist, pagan and Christian beliefs sometimes intermingled. Pagan rituals were modified to fit the new religion in an ecclesiastically acceptable manner. During the Christian Middle Ages the use of magiferous plants was sometimes flexible and sometimes restricted, but in the age of paganism, gods and heroes, plants and trees coexisted on many planes, both earthly and divine.

MEDITATION: YOUR PLACE IN TIME

Using herbs and plants and understanding their historical use is one way to connect with the energies of time, as is the exploration of ancient myth. The old ways are still relevant. We experience time as the by-product of planetary movement. Time has been deified as the Greek god Chronos, as well as personified as the patriarchal concept of Father Time. We intuitively seek to "make time" for things that are important to us, as if we were in control of this complex construct. In this meditation, you'll explore concepts of time. We are ruled by time in that our earthly lives have a beginning, a duration, and an end, much like all-natural organic matter on the planet. Our days are determined by the rotation of the sun on its axis, our years by the revolution of the earth around the sun. In between, we measure the fractions of minutes and moments that add up to a life of magick. Our time as individuals on earth is short. When compared to geologic time, our brief interlude seems infinitesimal. When compared to the lifespan of trees, our time on earth is still fleeting.

This does not mean it is insignificant. Often, we experience time through its scarcity. We say we are "running out of time" or that "time is slipping away from us" as if we had some semblance of control over this construct. Time is memory. It holds all the strands of our collective consciousness. Time is also the future; it is what we are moving through in order to get to our next destination. Think of yourself as an expression of time as you visualize your place along the continuum.

- Lie on your back with your knees bent and breathe deeply so that you are able to feel the expansion of breath across your lower back. Rest as much of your spine as you can on the earth and breathe into it. Close your eyes and imagine that you are feeling the turn of the earth; however, you are not turning sunwise, you are turning counterclockwise.

- Rotate the earth in your mind and picture yourself at this same time, only the day before. Observe yourself in the context of your recent past. What experiences have led you to the present moment? What was the high point from yesterday? What was the low point? Keep the sense of rotation in the forefront of your mind as you go back further. Picture the earth in relation to the sun, where it is today. See if you can envision it moving away from its present position into its previous position. Can you look at seasons past?

- Allow yourself to experience the past again. Bring to mind the people of influence, the temperature, and your state of mind. Observe the differences between then and now. Keep the image of the rotating earth in your mind and its position relative to the sun. Envision that it is now a year earlier. What has changed in this revolution around our nearest star? All the images and memories that you can conjure are still being projected into the vast reaches of space. You are experiencing time from a mutable point.

- You travel further back, greeting lost friends, growing younger with every passing year. Finally, you greet your parents as their child and still, you travel on, witnessing the origin of your current incarnation. As witness, you are able now to begin the observation of your elders and even your ancestors. You see your lineage unfolding before you as though you are traveling along the spiraling arms of the galaxy. Your distant past, the past that perhaps you have not previously accessed until now, is still projecting. You are simply meeting it at its origin point, as it is always flowing. Your distant past is still observable through the depths of space as a present moment somewhere. You are able to trace your bloodlines to their source, greet the love and struggle of thousands whose choices brought you to your present moment. You can see primeval forests, the land before human interference. You can observe the earth through geologic time, vast eras still changeable, as this is the only true constant.

- Continue to breathe as you create a paradigm shift in your visualization. Time stands still for a brief moment as you envision the earth turning sunwise again. You are able to experience all you have learned in reverse as a chronological narrative. You are able to remember places, faces, feelings, and voices. You find yourself lying comfortably in the present moment, the wealth of the past settling over you. You experience it as though it were the wind, fleeting, unmistakable, and unrepeatable. You experience time as though it were the current of a river, rushing by with purpose and power, never to retrace its path. You rotate the earth clockwise and see yourself in this same time and place tomorrow. You intuit your state of being and what you hope to gain incrementally between now and then.

Time As a Universal Creator

In the Orphic cult, time is personified by the god Chronos. The Orphic mystery religion has a distinct creation myth that posits that Chronos constructed an egg from which everything in existence emanated, first with the birth of Phanes, who took on the form of Eros, the god of love. Night was the daughter of love and consort of the god. From their union, all the life on earth and the stars in heaven were created. The image of the primal egg features in many creation accounts, including Homer's, while the accounts of Hesiod, who was synthesizing an anecdotal tradition, attributed the rise of the gods as a byproduct of Chaos; from the "yawning void" came the five original elements. They were the first gods; Gaia of the earth; Tartarus of the depths of the earth or underworld; Erebus, the gloom; Eros, the power of love; and Nyx or Night, the power of darkness.

- As you did before, only now in the opposite direction, spin and rotate the earth a year in the future. Observe with whom you have surrounded yourself, the manner of your dwelling, the activities in which you engage. Keep moving swiftly through time and place yourself in your future life. Can you picture the way you want it to be? Allow yourself the quiet peace to envision your idealized future of challenges accepted and met, obstacles overcome, ordeals completed, and joys enumerated with health, prosperity, and success intact. Picture it fully, and when your vision is clear, begin to speak aloud those future dreams that you most want to call into being, no matter how far away they seem right now.

RITUAL: THE VERBENAE AND THE VERBENARIUS

Verbena originally referred to twigs, foliage, and general herbage. It was a catch-all term to describe any number of woody flowering plants. The use of flowering plants was widespread in pagan rites. Wells were often decorated with wreaths on Sabbat festival days, and carrying flowering sprigs in procession was a significant part of pagan rites. A verbenae was a ritually prepared flower arrangement that was carried as an integral part of ritual procession preceding a rite, and the person chosen to carry it was given the honorary title of "Verbenarius." Creating a verbenae can add a layer of ancient authenticity to your practice. A verbenae can be part of a coven activity where members can take turns building and bearing the verbenae. The verbenae will also evolve over time and become part of the natural history of the group or individual who creates it.

1. Begin with a walk in the woods. Your walk can be silent and meditative as you take in the natural world around you. Walk with purpose to find a suitable stick that will serve as the base of your verbenae. The person charged with finding the base stick could be appointed the first Verbenarius who will begin the creative process and then nominate the next member to add on and bring the verbenae to future rituals. Specifically, you are looking for a walking stick, something with a minimum diameter of one and a half to two inches. Go out and seek, walk slowly and meditatively. Observe the world with a keen eye. You are searching for a ritual tool, something that will identify you as a solitary practitioner or that will resonate with your group. It should be strong and beautiful and not a burden to carry. Scan the ground. Look with mindful intent and purpose. You will know when you find it. If your search is in the grove where you gather or enact ritual, so much the better. Your verbenae will be an homage to your own piece of sacred ground. Bring an illustrated botanical guide of your regions with you so that you can identify the native plants around you and learn their properties. It is a disturbing fact of modern life that nearly everyone, including children, can identify

every corporate logo they encounter, but few are aware of the types of trees that grow in proximity to their homes. Take this as an opportunity to deepen your connection to nature.

2. Look for leafy boughs or flowering sprigs you can gather to decorate the verbenae. Feathers and interesting stones can also be added to make an ornate staff. Use colored ribbon or yarn to bind your found objects to the staff. You can even add amulets or talismans, even hanging crystals or pierced obsidian. Stones such as obsidian can be strung or wrapped with wire and then bound to the staff. These will make a delicate music when they touch. Be creative and artistic and reverent when you gather materials.

3. Lay out your finds either on your altar or in your grove. If you are part of a coven, encourage each member to contribute something emblematic of their magickal identity, such as a talisman, to add to the verbenae. When you have gathered sufficient material so that your verbenae will be decorative but not garish, with room to add on as the seasons change and the years progress, use this Roman pagan prayer to the Earth Goddess that comes from a twelfth-century medieval herbal:

"Hear, I beseech thee, and be favorable to my prayer.
Whatsoever herb thy power dost produce, give, I pray with
goodwill to all nations to save them and grant me this my medicine.
Come to me with thy powers, and howsoever I may use them may
they have good success and to whomsoever I may give them. Whatever
thou dost grant it may prosper. To thee all things return. Those who
rightly receive these herbs from me, do thou make them whole.
Goddess, I beseech thee; I pray thee as suppliant that by thy
majesty though grant this to me.

"Now I make intercession to you all ye powers and herbs and
to your majesty, ye whom Earth parent of all hath produced and given
as a medicine of health to all nations and hath put majesty upon you,
be, I pray you, the greatest help to the human race."

4. Prepare the staff by stripping off any outer bark and sanding with coarse sandpaper, 150–200 grit, revealing the wood beneath. Use a moistened cloth to remove the residual dust and allow the staff to dry. Prepare an essential oil blend as directed and thoroughly anoint the staff, imbuing it with herbal energy, a pleasing scent, and an enhancement to its appearance. This blend will be enough to cover a staff verbenae base that is approximately five to six feet tall and about two to three inches in diameter.

You will need:

- Glass for mixing
- Rubber gloves for mixing and application
- A square of cotton cloth or cosmetic cotton rounds
- Scent strips or wooden craft stick for mixing and scent preview
- Three and a half tablespoons of carrier oil such as fractionated organic coconut
- Twelve to fifteen drops of salvia officinalis sage essential oil
- Five drops of tea tree essential oil
- Two drops of lavender essential oil

Directions:

1. Carefully measure the carrier oil into a glass container. First add the sage essential oil and swirl them together. Add the tea tree and lavender and give them a stir with the scent strip. The aroma will be slightly medicinal, but this is a spiritually active calming and healing blend that makes an excellent anointing oil. While it is a little top-note heavy, this is appropriate because it is not designed to be worn on the skin, although it certainly can be. Feel free to anoint your pulse points to create the psychic bond between yourself and the ritual tool that you are making. Since the blend is top heavy, it will not linger on the skin for long.
2. Saturate the cotton with the oil and begin working it into the wood. Since your blend is complete with a carrier, you do not have to wear the gloves during this step, but you may if you find it more

comfortable to do so. While it can be a powerful attunement to use your bare hands to anoint, since this is a big project, you do not want to get overwhelmed. Essential oils even when blended are powerful natural elements and should be approached with respect and caution.

3. Once the base staff has been thoroughly anointed, you can begin arranging the decorations. Get input from your companions if you wish. Use the objects to tell a story. Include artifacts and mementos from past rituals intermixed with your found objects. Select colors with purpose. They can be expressions of individual or group magickal practice. Once your verbenae is complete, the first to initiate its creation should be named the First Verbenarius. The First Verbenarius will present the verbenae in a procession as the pagan ritual begins. This person should tell the narrative of its creation, the methods used, and any manifestations of divine affirmations that occurred during its creation. These can be recorded in the coven grimoire or the individual's book of shadows.

4. At the conclusion of the ritual, the next Verbernarius should be chosen by the first. The Second Verbenarius will take the verbenae home, protect it, anoint it, and add to its decoration and bring it to the next Sabbat or esbat. The verbenae can even be brought along on retreats or group excursions to mark campsites, territories, or individual families. Over time, its potency of natural magick will grow. You will find that as the years go by, having the verbenae in your home increases harmony. Additionally, appointing a Verbenarius can be a part of initiation or ordination preparation. Bestowing upon a coven member the role of Verbenarius means that she has to show up and participate, think, plan, and add on to this ancient and sacred ritual tool. She is responsible for its upkeep, its safe storage, and for bringing it to ritual. Think of ways to incorporate the ritual of the verbenae into your natural magick practice. One way is to use the verbenae to "beat the bounds" of the circle. After the directions and elements are invoked, the Verbenarius walks the boundary of the circle, striking the bottom of the staff along the ground with each step. The vibration creates a boundary and binds the practitioner to the land. There is much to be gained from the construction, maintenance, and bearing of the verbenae.

SPELL: THE SPIRAL OF TIME

At times, it is necessary to call upon ancestors for guidance. Ancestral work is an integral part of natural magick because it puts practitioners in touch with their familial patterns of migration and their connections to the wide span of the earth.

When you work with ancestral energy, there are certain things that you must understand and accept. Not every ancestral line exploration will bring harmony. Many people have destruction buried in their lineage of which they may or may not be aware. Be prepared to meet your bloodline with honesty. Craft your spells to confront and heal the energy signature of the past. After all, you are the culmination of your many bloodlines. Every choice your ancestors made ultimately led to you. You are the distilled essence of their love and also their struggles. Honor what is honorable and accept the power to change any ancestral deeds that were less than honorable. Death does not immediately bestow benevolence on a discarnate spirit. This spell will enable you to better integrate ancestral energy into your natural magickal practice.

You will need:

- An ancestral photo to place upon the altar
- Sprigs of rosemary, fresh if available; otherwise, dried herbs will suffice
- Pomegranate seeds if you are in the season of Mabon or Samhain
- A black votive candle in a jar or glass, anointed and dressed if you prefer
- Incense preferably made by you (frankincense, clove, and myrrh would be appropriate choices)
- A crystal ball for gazing
- A black gauze cloth or lace veil

Directions:

1. Set upon your altar the photograph in a frame so that it stands upright. On both sides of the photograph, place a sprig of rosemary.

If you are using dried needles, place two small bundles, one on each side, or leave the needles out in a small dish or two. The pomegranate seeds should be on the altar as an offering to the dead. You may also substitute any known preferred food in place of the symbolic offering if you have need to call upon your ancestors at a time other than the waning year. In front of the photograph, place the candle. The candle may be inscribed with significant dates or symbols that relate to the lineage with which you wish to attune, amplify, or heal.

2. Before beginning your spell, make sure that your intention is clear in your mind. State out loud the wish you seek. Some grounds for spellcasting could include:

- Honoring your ancestors
- Healing a rift from an old transgression
- Asking your ancestors for aid in a specific endeavor

3. After stating your intention, burn the incense upon your altar and transition yourself into a meditative state. Begin envisioning your family history as far back as you are able. From what lands did your ancestor emigrate? What were their modes of transportation? What were their challenges? Which did they overcome? If you do not have the facts, open your mind and allow yourself to intuit the vision of how you came to be. What were the catalysts that led to this moment in time? You may feel a little nudge or physical sensation when your ancestors are present. When you receive the affirmation, light the candle.

4. Place the crystal ball in front of the candle and drape the photograph so that it is veiled. You are acknowledging the separation between you and the lineage of your past as you focus on the light passing through the crystal. The veil represents the separation. The crystal is the lens through which you will interact with the energy signature that you are given. You must meet them where they are; on the other side of the veil, the unknowable river, which you may touch but not cross until you meet your own end of days. Call to them and ask them to lend energy to your spell

that you may achieve your goals. Speak the names of those who make themselves known to you. Ask for their blessing and their aid, or alternately as the case may be, offer them your forgiveness. Whatever you seek, do it in earnest and articulate it clearly.

5. Reach out and touch the crystal. Rest your fingertips gently upon it to deepen the connection you have established. Be mindful and present in the moment. Allow the candle to burn down as you observe its light through the crystal. Open your mind to messages, visions, and insights. Record what you have learned. You may extinguish the candle at the end of your spell, but leave the seeds out for your ancestors to take their essence. Return them to nature the next day; do not partake of them yourself.

CHARM: ANCIENT HERBAL CHARMS

The use of herbal charms as protection has survived from antiquity until today. You can attune with ancient energies by constructing an herbal charm from the same ingredients used by ancient pagans. The natural world is in a constant state of renewal, and so we should all be able to take the gifts of the past and integrate them into modern natural magick. One way to effectively achieve this is through simplicity. A bright flower and a fresh leaf bound together with a bit of magick can exert any amount of desirable influence on the world today. Remember, historically it was through human agency that the magiferous plants acquired their miraculous powers, and these powers were neither inherent nor permanent. They arose out of the connection between the natural world and the natural magician. These charms are based upon authentic medieval charms.

Protective Herbal Charm

Take the blossom of a marigold and place a thorn on the blossom. Wrap the flower with bay laurel leaves and tie together with white ribbon or yarn. If you cannot obtain fresh bay laurel, you may substitute dried bay laurel; soak or stem them first in order to make them pliable. Do this when the moon is full and keep the charm wrapped in white cloth bound with red ribbon, yarn, or cord. Keep it close by until your results have been achieved. When you release the charm, return it to your garden or your grove.

Herbal Charm to Eliminate Unwanted Dreams

Gather a small bundle of vervain and rosemary. Bind them together with gold-colored or metallic thread. Make a sachet by putting the bundled herbs in a muslin pouch. Place the sachet under your pillow as you sleep for seven consecutive nights on the waning moon.

Time for Spells

In casting a spell, candles are often used. In an ideal situation, the witch would be able to let the candle burn down in its entirety; however, this is not always possible. It has become customary for witches to manipulate time in the following way: just as a candle burning its course aids the power of the spell, the results can be hastened by pushing a needle as far down into the wick of the candle as it can go. The incantation is then revised to reflect that the spell is considered carried out when the flame reaches the needle.

Chapter Eleven

AWARENESS AS A MAGICKAL ENDEAVOR

The Realm of Self

It takes time and dedication to become adept at natural magick. Within the realm of the self, the natural magick practitioner begins to see individuality within the greater context of its relationship to divinity and to the natural world and the many places where these intersect. You may find that aspects of your own personality resonate with ancient descriptions of archetypal deities. You may share a physical resemblance to archaeological representations of the goddess. The emblems and symbols of deity may even be your own. You may discover that the owl, long associated with the goddess Athena, is one of your spirit animals. You may find that when performing magick, you notice the presence of a spider, which leads you to discover the mythology of Sussitenako, Kokyangwute, or Na'ashjéii Asdzáá, the Spider Woman of the Native American tradition. You might experience a déjà vu when visiting a place of power or a ley line crossing, a feeling that the place is energetically familiar even if it is new to you. As you attune more and more to the natural world, pausing to hear the sound that an autumn leaf makes when it touches the ground or to feel the rush of a river current across your body, you begin to understand the self as a collection of elements, minerals, organic matter, and water. You deepen your connection to history, to the wisdom of the ancients. You accept that like the deities, the forces of nature are powerful and distinct, commanding respect and the use of wisdom and good judgment, and require ethical dealings with your fellow denizens of earth.

In the Wiccan Rede, there is much emphasis placed on the last two lines, "Eight words the Wiccan Rede fulfill: And it harm none, do what thou will." Many practitioners use this last couplet as a replacement for the entire Rede, making the assumption that the "thou" in the last line refers to the individual practitioner, without considering the fact that it is also a pact with elemental energies and the goddesses and gods. It is not only an invocation of personal agency; it is a plea for a harmonious and divine exchange of energy over which the practitioner admits no direct control. It is unlikely that powerful elemental beings will arrive when called to do your bidding if you have not first been listening very carefully, interacting with nature appropriately, and invoking correctly.

Expand your range of sensory perception. With so many demands for our time and attention, it is easy to let something as important as self-awareness fall by the wayside. Throughout these pages, we have sought to deepen our connection to the natural world through the use of natural magick. It is time to turn these techniques inward so that we may benefit from the potency of our acquired wisdom. Whether our needs include influencing an outcome or personal healing, using natural magick can enhance our spellcraft and heighten our powers of perception. Witches are natural healers, calling upon the forces of nature to inform and empower their work.

The earliest concepts of medical care connected the human body to the elements, and herbs were used to address imbalances. The four bodily "humors," the sanguine, phlegmatic, choleric, and melancholic, were believed to keep an individual in good health when they were balanced. An imbalance of the humors signified illness. The elements of earth, air, fire, and water were connected to the physical states of being hot, dry, moist, or cold. The bodily humors reflected the understanding of the root of illnesses during the fifth century B.C.E. Imbalance of the humors was treated with herbs, the most important and often only type of medical care from ancient pagan civilization through the Christian Middle Ages. Active ingredients contained in herbs are still in use today. Homeopathic practice is one example of the enduring efficacy of herbs and how we can tap into their natural abilities to heal. Furthermore, elemental beings are also connected to the sensory perceptions of practitioners of natural magick. Air is the corresponding element to hearing, while sight is associated with fire. Water represents the sense of taste, and touch belongs to earth. Think of the five senses you were conditioned to believe that you have, and now consider how many more you already possess in which you were never formally instructed. In addition to sight, hearing, taste, touch, and smell, you have probably noticed that you also have a sense of balance, speed, elevation, and temperature. Most people are versed in the concept of having five senses without realizing that they may have twenty or more. Add to the list a range of psychic abilities and intuition, and you can see how sensory perception can expand exponentially. Begin to trust what you feel and know to be correct.

MEDITATION: THE POWER OF THE PENTAGRAM

There is perhaps no other symbol as highly charged or as misinterpreted as the pentacle. The pentacle is widely used in witchcraft for a variety of spells, including invoking, banishing, shielding, protecting, and receiving, as well as representing the dual nature of practitioners. This dual nature can best be expressed as the belief that humanity is a pinnacle of natural existence. We have an animal nature that coexists with divine awareness. The pentacle represents many things, among them the pinnacle of humanity and the sum of creation as it appears within the divine order of the universe. This order is evident in nature.

The pentagram always conforms to the "golden section" or the "golden cut," as it is also known. This is a ratio that can be expressed as 1:1.618. It is this pattern that governs so much of the beauty found in the natural world. We see it in the arrangement of sunflower seeds, which radiate outwardly in two spirals going in opposite directions. It appears in the arrangement of leaves of the artichoke and the pineapple. It is the same pattern that produces the spiral of the pinecone's scales and the shell of the chambered nautilus. The golden section informs the patterns of ferns and other plants, the human body, and the nature of animals. This predictable and oft-repeating pattern of numbers, called the Fibonacci sequence, was named for Fibonacci Leonardo of Pisa (c. 1175–c. 1250), who discovered that the rate at which rabbits in captivity multiply was also 1:1.1618. This ratio led to an entire field of study dedicated to the patterns of plant growth in nature and how they are informed upon by the golden section. Phyllotaxis, as it is called, is almost cultlike with the passion of its advocates.

How the pentacle interacts with the human body is interesting to note. In appearance, it resembles the human form with a head and four appendages. A perfect pentagon can be made by connecting each point of the pentacle to each other with a straight line. In the center of the pentacle, another pentagon will appear. Pentacles also have a musicality about them; they seem to want to dance with each other. If you draw a series of pentacles, each one touching one point of the one next to it, they will form a perfect circle. The magickal associations of the pentacle within the circle are obvious. In nature, there are undeniable connections and patterns as well that are also reflected in the human form. The ratio of the human hand to the arm from the inside of the elbow to the wrist is around 1:1.618. Further examination of the body reveals that the foot also fits perfectly inside this section of the forearm, making the relationship between the hands, compared to the arms, and feet the same.

Place a pentacle within a circle and you will create the pentagram, a potent magickal symbol. Arrange the pentagram with the point facing up, and you will have the resemblance of the human form encircled within the harmony of the universe. Invert the pentagram, and the horns of the god are seen: the wild animal nature that also dwells in us all. People unfamiliar with natural magick often fear the inverted pentagram because they do not understand it. Natural magick does not give power to demons. The upward-facing points that we see represent the untamed forces of nature, the animal spirits of hoof and horn. This duality of human nature exists. Practitioners of natural magick embrace their wild side, their natural instincts. Instead of being cut off from nature, nature is embraced in all its power and fury. This can be terrifying to the uninitiated. Highly charged symbols should be carefully guarded and used with care.

In this meditation, we will explore the dual nature and use of the pentagram.

- Begin with a cyclical breathing technique, inhaling deeply to a count of five, holding the breath for a count of five, exhaling slowly for a count of five, and holding again for a count of five, before repeating the pattern. With each cycle of breath, envision a pentacle, a perfect five-pointed star, and hold the picture in your mind. As you continue to breathe, envision in your mind another pentacle with its "arm" touching the first one. Continue to envision and breathe until you can complete the circle of pentacles in your mind.

- When the circle is complete, train your mind to see the linked pentacles as a whole and complete entity. Use your psychic vision to zoom out until the details of what comprises your circle are undiscernible. In your mind's eye, you now hold the vision of the circle, but in your heart you know that the circle is made up of individual pentacles. Now envision within the circle another pentacle. You have created the pentagram, the meeting place of humanity and the plant and animal world, where existence is formed in wondrous perfection that follows the proportion of the universe itself.

- Begin to rotate the pentagram slowly in your mind. Notice if you experience the presence of any colors. You may see the image of Leonardo da Vinci's *Vitruvian Man*, that paragon of human proportional perfection. Allow the pentagram to turn sunwise until it is inverted. Here you may see the face of Pan, the horned god of the forest. At this point, you will change your breathing technique to the breath of fire, deep varying breaths of unpredictable duration. Allow the wild energy of the forest, the hunt, the flight of deer, the wildness of goats, the leap of the stag to inform your thoughts. *Pan* is the root of the word "panic," a state of frenzy, arousal, passion, and unpredictability. Allow yourself to feel unrestrained energy. Imagine yourself untethered from any manmade constraints.

The Sacred Geometry of the Golden Section

In sacred geometry, which gives mathematical explications of the divine order of the universe, the golden section is expressed as the Greek letter Phi: Φ. Phi is used because it is the initial of Phidias, the Athenian sculptor and architect of the Parthenon. Some of Phidias's most famous works include the three sculptures of the goddess Athena that adorned the Acropolis. They are known as *Athena Promachos*, the *Lemnian Athena*, and the *Athena Parthenos*.

- Put yourself in a natural place with all that it entails: the wind and rain, the starkness of the earth, the rush of river currents, the heat of the flame. Continue the chaotic breathing pattern while you meditate on this duality of nature. Turn the pentagram again and find yourself upright, back in your human form. You are wise and in control, aware of your animal nature, but not ruled by it. You are but one in a sea of stars, each with its unique gift and purpose. Return to the four-part cycle of controlled breathing and holding to a count of five. As you breathe deeply and peacefully, allow your vision to zoom in. Once again, you find yourself within a circle of stars, forever dancing with joy at the divine perfection of the universe and your own place within it.

RITUAL: WITCHES BREW: CREATING TEAS AND TONICS

Witches are healers, and when it comes to practicing the healing arts, there is no better person to start with than yourself, and no better teacher than herbs. Food-grade quality herbs are very safe and will not hurt you. These tonic herbs are to be used in moderation and with the understanding that anything in large and inappropriate quantities (even water) can be harmful. Any contraindications, such as allergies you may have or medications that you are taking, should be thoroughly investigated before you begin experimenting with tonic herbs. Herbs are powerful and potent. The practice of herbalism varies in different regions around the world. In this chapter, the emphasis will be on Western Herbal Medicine. The primary types of herbalism practiced in the world include:

- **Western Herbal Medicine:** As its name implies, Western Herbal Medicine is derived from Western Europe and is practiced in France, England, Italy, Poland, and Germany, where herbalists are licensed and recognized. In France, aromatherapy is a recognized medicinal practice. It is worth noting that in the United States of America, herbal medicine is not a licensed profession, nor is there any legal definition of what an herbalist is or does.

- **Traditional Chinese Medicine:** Traditional Chinese Medicine, or TCM, is taught in acupuncture schools and is very different from Western Herbal Medicine. Traditional Chinese Medicine has been in use for more than five thousand years.
- **Ayurvedic:** Ayurvedic herbalism originates from India. An ancient practice, Ayurveda is centered on balance and built on the philosophy that each herb, plant, animal, or mineral has a specific energy signature, as well as specific properties in different proportions. These qualities include heat, cold, heaviness, and lightness of twenty different types. Health is viewed as a harmonic interaction between the mind, body, and spirit.

Other forms of herbalism include homeopathy, aromatherapy, and Bach Flower Remedies. Homeopathic herbalism uses the philosophy of treating "like with like" to heal the body. Most preparations involve minute amounts of herbal material. Similarly, Bach Flower Remedies contain an essence of an herb in a diluted solution. Aromatherapy is the only one of these three that involves chemistry. Many people are skeptical of the efficacy of flower remedies and homeopathy due to their diluted composition, comparing their effectiveness to placebos. However, it is important to recognize that even while lacking in plant chemistry, these herbal preparations are able to serve as a catalyst for healing to take place in many people. To discount this phenomenon as a placebo effect is to deny the power of the mind to heal the body. This is the realm where true natural magick lies, when the desired outcome cannot be attributed to anything other than the will of the practitioner.

Types of Herbal Preparations

Herbs can be used in a variety of ways, including teas and tonics, tinctures, and topical treatments such as salves and creams. Teas and tonics are easy and relatively fast to prepare, but have a short shelf life. Tinctures last much longer and require much smaller doses. Topical treatments are used directly on the skin and are never eaten or taken internally. There are three main "flavors" of herbs. They are:

1. Tonic herbs
2. Medicinal herbs
3. Poisons

Tonic herbs are safe to consume even in large quantities and can be used continuously without any adverse effects. Tonic herbs can be eaten. Some examples of tonic herbs are basil, dandelion, peppermint, rosehips, and chickweed. Medicinal herbs are stronger and are not for continuous use. Medicinal herbs such as *Echinacea purpurea*, goldenseal, licorice, berberine, and wild cherry bark can be used for a period of four to six weeks, after which you should wait at least three weeks before returning to their use. Herbs such as *Echinacea* and goldenseal have antibiotic properties, and their effectiveness declines with continued use. Poisons are highly toxic and are only used under the supervision of a medical doctor. Some examples of poisons are foxglove, which slows the heart, and opium poppies, from which morphine is derived.

From Tonic to Tea

Tonic herbs can be made into tea. A cup of tea made from a tea bag is not a tonic; it is a beverage. The amount of herbs in herbal tea is too small and the time required for steeping is not nearly long enough to extract the desired effect from the herbs. A cup of herbal tea can be pleasing and comforting, but it is very different from creating a healing herbal tea. Tea is also a specific plant. Different types of tea are often just referring to the different methods of gathering and drying, as well as the different parts of the tea plant that are used. For example, green tea is made from the lightly steamed leaves of the tea plant. White tea refers to a beverage made from the new tender leaves. A black tea means that the leaves were both steamed and fermented. What we purchase when we buy "loose tea" is actually the waste and byproducts left over from herbs that are processed into tea bags.

For a tea or tonic to have a nutritional or medicinal benefit, the plant material must be water-soluble and steeped for enough time for extraction to occur. The types of teas explained here are actually herbal tonics that can be safely used for general wellness. The

Western Herbalism methods will be explored so that you can gain understanding of the safe herbs associated with wellness, their properties and effects, and their preparation.

How to Choose an Herb

When you first encounter dried herbs, it doesn't matter if you have foraged or gardened or purchased them. You will still need to judge their quality before deciding what and how to use them. A dry herb should resemble its living counterpart. You are looking for four basic qualities:

1. Color
2. Smell
3. Taste
4. Effect

An herb will retain its original color if it was dried properly. Herbs will speak to you, and you will gain knowledge of their use through their taste. Some of the herbal qualities associated with taste are:

- **Sweet:** Sweet-tasting herbs are nourishing. They calm the nerves and act as tissue builders and balance sugar.
- **Salty:** Salty herbs contain mineral salt. They are nutritive and high in vitamins and minerals. Salty herbs include seaweed and oatstraw.
- **Spicy:** Spicy herbs can dry up mucous and stimulate circulation. Spicy herbs are activating. Ginger is an example of a spicy herb.
- **Bitter:** Bitter herbs affect digestion.
- **Sour:** Sour herbs are balancing to the tissues. They contain vitamins and minerals. Lemon and wood sorrel are sour herbs.

Herbs that have long-term beneficial effects are called alteratives. Alteratives such as red clover, dandelion, and burdock can be used for cleansing and wellness. Different herbs will have different effects on the body if the herbs are prepared into a tea or tonic and consumed. It is important to familiarize yourself with the specific part of the herb that is used. Different *parts* of the herb will also have different effects. Some of the effects of herbal energies include warming, cooling, moistening, and drying. A drying effect would be a good choice if you have a runny nose, while a cooling effect can address hot flashes. Herbs also have digestive actions. Bitter herbs help digest fat by increasing bile. Carminative herbs are high in volatile oils and increase peristalsis, which can reduce gas. Carminative herbs can also decrease the amount of time it takes to digest food. Antispasmodic herbs can alleviate cramps, while demulcent herbs add moisture. Conversely, astringent herbs remove moisture, which is helpful in addressing issues such as diarrhea. Here are a few examples:

Examples of Bitter Herbs
- German Chamomile
- Arugula
- Artichoke Leaf
- Dandelion

Examples of Carminative Herbs
- Lavender
- Ginger
- Peppermint
- German Chamomile

Examples of Antispasmodic Herbs
- Wild Yam
- Red Clover
- Valerian Root
- Fennel

Examples of Demulcent Herbs
- Marshmallow
- Slippery Elm
- Violet Leaf

Preparation

An herbal tonic can be made from any part of a plant, including the leaves, stems, roots, flowers, fruits, berries, or bark. Herbs can and do heal! Different parts require different preparation methods; however, one variable will affect all parts: whether you are using fresh or dried plant material.

- If you are using fresh plants, you should fill your container to the top.
- If you are using dried plant material, fill your container only halfway.

There are two preparation methods of herbal tea. These are:

- Infusion
- Decoction

When preparing an herbal infusion, fill your container, such as a glass mason jar or a French press, with fresh herbs, or half full with dried herbs. In a kettle or pot, bring fresh spring water to a boil, then pour over the herbs, allowing them to steep. If you are using leaves, plan to let them steep for four to six hours. If you are using flowers, they will only need to steep for twenty to thirty minutes. Infusions are best for the "aerial" parts of the plant: the leaves, stems, and flowers that are exposed to the air.

Identifying Medicinal Herbs

Every plant has a specific scientific name that identifies that particular plant and never refers to any other variety. Latin names were adopted to ease communication between scientific communities across countries and cultures. Each scientific name contains the genus and species expressed in Latin. When you encounter an herb with the word "officinale" in its name, this is an indicator that the plant has a medicinal action and was part of the original herbal pharmacopeia.

If you are using bark or roots, you need to decoct. Roots and bark have rigid cell walls that take additional time and heat to break down. It helps to chop up the material before decocting. The only exception to this is if you are using a highly aromatic bark that is high in volatile oils. If this is the case, use the steep time for flowers and berries. You can tell if a root or bark is high in volatile oils by the smell. Ginger root is an example of a root high in volatile oil. Peppermint is another. Also, when using roots, you will need to only fill your container half full, no matter if they are fresh or dried.

Decoction is done over a period of two to four hours over constant heat. There are many ways you can do this. One way is to use the stovetop, keeping the heat very low, monitoring frequently, and allowing the herbs to simmer slowly. If you cannot monitor, you can use a slow cooker to decoct herbs. Additionally, in order to keep the herbs hot for the longer period of time that decocting requires, you can use a coffeepot.

After your herbs have steeped for the appropriate amount of time, you will need to strain them. One way to do this is to use a French press, which has a built-in strainer. It can be slightly difficult because the saturated herbs have a tendency to stick to the sides of the pot, making it hard to press them down. Another method is to pour the contents into another clean sterilized container through a sieve, strainer, or cheesecloth to catch the plant material, leaving the infused liquid for use. The saved liquid will last for three to four days, and it can be reheated. You can enjoy up to three cups a day, but remember your reasons for creating the preparation in the first place. Bitter herbs will taste bitter and if you add a sweetener, you will cancel out their digestive benefit.

Brewing and Blending

While it is fine to begin working with just a single plant to observe its effects, you may want to start creating your own herbal tea blends. You can do this by first identifying the overall or primary effect you want your blend to have. Then, choose one or two secondary herbs that will have a harmonizing effect. They can either affect the taste to make it more pleasant or have a nutritive or healing benefit.

HEALING HERBS		
Herb Name	*Scientific Name*	*Effect*
Burdock	*Arctium lappa*	Burdock is a detoxifying herb that is effective in treating skin conditions such as acne and rashes.
Chamomile	*Matricaria chamomile*	A mildly relaxing herb, chamomile is a helpful remedy for addressing stress and anxiety.
Dandelion	*Taraxacum officinale*	High in potassium, dandelion also aids digestion and cleanses the liver.
Echinacea	*Echinacea purpurea*	*Echinacea* boosts the immune system. It is an alternative herb and has antibiotic properties.
Ginger	*Zingiber officinale*	Ginger promotes good circulation. It is a warming herb and also alleviates nausea.
Green Tea	*Camellia sinensis*	High in antioxidants, green tea promotes calmness and a sense of peace.
Lavender	*Lavandula officinalis*	Relaxing to the body, lavender also has antibacterial and antifungal properties.
Lemon Balm	*Melissa officinalis*	Relaxing and anti-spasmodic, lemon balm boosts the immune system and is anti-inflammatory.
Lemon Verbena	*Aloysia citrodora*	Often used in cooking, lemon verbena relieves bloating and calms a nervous stomach.
Mugwort	*Artemisia vulgaris*	Sometimes called cronewort, mugwort is high in calcium and can help bring on menses.
Nettle	*Urtica dioica*	An important tonic for women, nettle is high in vitamins and minerals such as calcium, iron, and vitamins A, C, and K.
Oatstraw	*Avena sativa*	High in calcium and very nourishing, oatstraw is a demulcent and relieves nervous exhaustion.

HEALING HERBS		
Herb Name	**Scientific Name**	**Effect**
Passionflower	*Passiflora incarnata*	Relaxing to the nervous system, passion-flower has sedative effects.
Red Clover	*Trifolium praetense*	Red clover aids the symptoms of menopause and also protects the liver and lungs. It is also a mild sedative.
Rose	*Rosa centifolia*	Healing and soothing, rose relaxes the heart and is also used as an aphrodisiac.
Scullcap	*Scutellaria lateriflora*	A relaxing nervine, skullcap can also be used for mild pain relief and for nourishing the nervous system.
Spearmint	*Mentha gracilis*	Ideal for cold relief, spearmint is a stimulant as well as a digestive aid and blends well with other herbs.

When creating a blend, plan on making 70–75 percent of the content from your primary herb and the remaining 25–30 percent from the harmonizing herb. Keep notes to record your experiences so that you can adjust your blend and make it optimal. Also, keeping notes will allow you to recreate successful blends.

As you grow more confident, you may want to concoct more complex blends. Knowledge of herbal energetics is important when creating complex blends. A complex blend will have either a tonic or medicinal purpose and will include three actions, such as astringent, carminative, or bitter. Think about your wellness needs. For example, you may want to create a sleep aid and stress reducer with a digestive benefit. Think of what your primary herb should be and which other two herbs will accomplish the other needs. Mix the herbs together in a stainless steel or glass bowl and then infuse or decoct, depending on the material.

Working with herbs will keep you humble. There are more than fifteen thousand different genera of plants, making it impossible to know them all. Experiment with safe tonic herbs and tap into their benefits. Witches are healers, and using herbs safely and wisely is an extension of natural magick.

SPELL: THE ART OF SELF CARE, LOVE, AND ACCEPTANCE

Each of us has a genuine desire to attune with something greater than ourselves during times of distress. At times it seems we are constantly bombarded with negativity, and remaining hopeful and confident feels like a task too great to bear. Unattainable images of perfection are endlessly splashed across our psyches in an attempt to debase the individual worth of a person and convince her that happiness and fulfillment lie just around the corner with the next purchase, the new product, the latest convenience.

Natural magick allows us to shed the obligation to superficial perfection. In the charge of the goddess, we hear wisdom from the source: "If that which you seek you do not find within, you will never find it without." Happiness does not radiate from the external; its flow is from the internal toward the external, and never the other way around. There is nothing outside of you that can "make" you happy, for you are the creatrix and architect of your own life and path. Self-care and acceptance, embracing your true self and being honest about who you are instead of whom you believe society wishes you to be, is a powerful affirmation. In classical Greece, healing cults arose in response to the human desire to invoke spiritual agency to heal the body and the spirit. You can adapt the ancient practices of self-care to address your own immediate needs, creating personal natural magick inspired by antiquity.

1. Begin with an effigy candle. This can be a sculpted candle or a jar candle carved with your own symbology. If you are using a jar candle, inscribe it with your name in the Theban alphabet, a sigil of your own design, or you can use the elemental triangles. Include your date of birth and astrological insignia.

2. Anoint the candle with essential oil of gardenia or something that pleases you. You can add crushed copal or another resin that you prefer to bring out either the carvings or the features of your anointed candle. Use a bit of the oil (if it is combined with a dilutant) on your third eye chakra center, in the middle of your

forehead. Place an altar cloth of your favorite color out with a chalice of fresh water and a stick of incense.

3. Use the water to perform a self-blessing after you light the candle. Begin by dipping your fingers in the water and anointing your forehead, your lips, heart, sex, and feet. Light a favorite incense and listen to it for the duration of its burning.

RITUAL ASCLEPIEIA: HONORING HYGEIA

Hygeia was one of the daughters of Asclepius, the most prominent god of healing in classical Greece. Many gods and goddesses assumed the tasks of healing, including Artemis, who was the keeper of pregnant women, infants, and young children, while Athena was also worshipped as Athena Hygeia on the Acropolis. Healing cults practiced their arts at sacred places, not wholly unlike the retreat centers of today. The most well-preserved healing locations, including Amphiareion near Oropus and the Asclepieia in Epidarus and Kos, contain several consistent central features. Both had a sanctuary dedicated to deity, an incubation hall, a bath, a theater, and guest lodging. Healing was done through incubation, the ritual of sleeping in the sanctuary. First, an offering was made by the person seeking healing, then a physical cleansing took place in the ritual baths. Afterward, the practitioner would lie down in the "koimeterion," a long hall, compartmentalized with many sleeping chambers. Visions of the deity would appear, often with an accompanying animal, such as a snake or a dog, as both animals were emblematic of healing. These animals would interact with the practitioner in their dreams, sometimes licking or even biting a specific place on the body most in need of healing. Votive offerings, sometimes of silver or gold, were placed in the temple.

1. Begin with a purification rite of your own design. Think of the things in your psyche, the Greek word for soul, that need strengthening. If you are harboring any self-doubt, use the purification rite to release yourself from the expectations of others. If you are feeling a drain on your energy, try to identify the source and release yourself from its hold over you. Breathe deeply and

freely, allowing yourself this time to get in touch with yourself, your needs, and your desires.

2. Upon your altar, place a bouquet of healing herbs and a few votive candles. Let there also be an image of a snake or a dog. This can be a photograph, an effigy of your own making, or a small sculpture or trinket. Place a chalice of fresh water there as well so that elemental harmony and balance are well represented. Focus on the lighted candles and envision yourself in a place of peace. Allow yourself to let go of your shortcomings for the moment; with each exhalation of breath, release the disappointments that cloud your vision. With each intake of breath, create an image of wholeness and fulfillment in your mind. Think of yourself as the perfect being inside of the never-ending circle that embraces the pentagram. See yourself for who you truly are and feel the attainment of your highest self. When your dream is clear, blow out the candles and with the release of breath, think of the fire radiating out into the universe, your petition delivered to the feet of the goddess in whom you trust to deliver it to the exact right place in the cosmic web of time and space.

3. Prepare a ritual bath for yourself, using everything you have learned. Bring the candles with you if you desire. Perfume the air with an aromatherapy spray and let healing steaming herbs infuse the water. Soak and relax until the water turns tepid, then prepare yourself for sleep. Use your aromatherapy spray on your bed linens and dress mindfully as if you are preparing not just for sleep, but for an astral journey that will bring you an encounter with divine energy. Take the herbs from your altar and put them in a sachet underneath your pillow. Keep your grimoire close to your bedside so that you may scribe your dreams upon waking in the morning.

CHARM: PERSONAL AMULETS AND TALISMANS

Much in the same way as a mantra can put a practitioner of magick into a trancelike or meditative state, so too can creating a personal talismanic amulet enhance the experience of practicing natural magick.

You will need to become adept with symbology and try your hand in a new form of creativity. Draw upon what you have learned from this book in regards to herbs with which you resonate, animals with which you feel connection, elements that manifest readily for you, and the planetary symbols that correspond with your sun sign or rising sign, as well as your astrological emblems. You can synthesize these highly personal symbols into a talisman that is linked to your energy signature. Its purpose is to remind you of your true nature and to amplify your individuality. A talisman can be worn as part of ceremonial garb for ritual or it can be a part of your daily devotional practice. You should create the talisman using natural elements, and it should not be handled or touched by any person other than yourself.

1. Begin with a self-study and touch upon the symbols that will benefit you the most. You can sketch or outline them in your grimoire. Next, think about the material you want to use. Clay is easy to work with and can be readily obtained at craft stores. Some riverbanks have clay that can be collected and manipulated, then dried. Think about the silhouette and what geometric outline suits you best. Would your talisman be round, flat, or spherical? Do you want an oblong design similar to the Egyptian cartouche? Maybe you are interested in using the principle of sacred geometry and want to create a pentagram outline. Think of the negative space and how many symbols you can include and how they relate to each other. Also consider if you are planning to wear your talisman or carry it in a pouch. If your intent is to wear it, you will need to fashion it with a hole. If you make the hole from front to back, you will have to add a connecting ring through the hole so that your talisman does not hang sideways. An east-west perforation can be difficult to craft unless the material you are using is thick enough to provide stability. Also consider what type of cord you will use and if it will have any type of clasp. It can be frustrating to get to the end of creating a talisman only to discover that your chain or cord is too thick to pass through. It is a good practice to think of the mechanics at the beginning rather than the end.

The Modern Witchcraft Book of Natural Magick

2. If you are using clay, you can even press botanicals into the material while it is soft. Small leaves and flower petals add a natural element to your inscriptions. A toothpick or bamboo skewer can make a good stylus for engraving symbols into crafting clay. After it is thoroughly dry, you can paint it or leave it plain. Wear it, use it as an altar object, or keep it in a medicine pouch as a touchstone for times when you need to remind yourself of your unique abilities and to get in touch with your creative side.

Chances are, by now you have come to realize that you have been practicing some form of natural magick your entire life. When you first blew out a birthday candle with the intention of wish fulfillment, you aligned breath with fire to call a desire into being. If you ever picked a dandelion that had gone to seed and made a wish as you blew upon the fluffy seeds to set them in flight, you practiced air and herb magick. If you ever wished upon a falling star, you looked to a celestial event to lend its aid to the manifestation of your will.

Look at your instincts and actions, and perhaps you will be surprised to discover that natural magick lives up to its name in that it comes naturally. As you learn to trust your instincts more and more, you will find delightful correlations between science and spirituality, that the laws of nature and of magick coexist quite harmoniously and without contradiction. You may find yourself wanting to pursue natural magick even deeper, through advanced herbalism, earth science, water conservation, permaculture, astronomy, and the like. Remember that magick must always be ethical, and whatever we do to the earth, we ultimately do to ourselves. Let the pure beauty of your magickal self-inform your choices so that they may harm none and be of benefit to all beings. So mote it be. Merry meet and merry part and merry meet again.

Appendix

RESOURCES

For bottles and supplies referenced in Chapters 4, 6, and 11, Specialty Bottle is recommended: www.specialtybottle.com.

For essential oils in bulk, Jedwards International, Inc., is recommended: https://bulknaturaloils.com.

For organic herbs, Mountain Rose Herbs is recommended: www.mountainroseherbs.com.

SELECTED BIBLIOGRAPHY

"Pythagoras and the Music of the Spheres," www.dartmouth .edu/~matc/math5.geometry/unit3/unit3.html.

Ascalone, Enrico. *Mesopotamia*. University of California Press. 2005.

Bach, Edward. *The Twelve Healers and Other Remedies*. The Bach Center. 1941.

Barringer, Judith M. *Divine Escorts: Nereids in Archaic and Classical Greek Art.* University of Michigan Press. 1995.

Bogard, Paul. *The Ground Beneath Us.* Hachette Book Group. 2017.

Carr-Gomm, Philip and Richard Heygate. *The Book of English Magic.* The Overlook Press. 2010.

Chronicle Books, pub. *A Medieval Herbal.* 1994.

Emoto, Masaru. *The Secret Life of Water.* Simon & Schuster. 2006.

Fidler, J. Havelock. *Ley Lines: Their Nature and Properties.* Turnstone Press Limited. 1984.

Graves, Robert. *The White Goddess.* Farrar, Straus and Giroux. 1966.

Green, Marian. *The Elements of Natural Magic.* Element Books Limited. 1989.

Hamilton, Edith. *Mythology: Timeless Tales of Gods and Heroes.* Little, Brown and Company. 1969.

Littleton, C. Scott, ed. *Mythology: The Illustrated Anthology of World Myth and Storytelling.* Thunder Bay Press. 2002.

Michell, John with Allan Brown. *How the World Is Made: The Story of Creation According to Sacred Geometry.* Thames & Hudson Limited. 2009.

Morita, Kiyoko. *The Book of Incense: Enjoying the Traditional Art of Japanese Scents.* Kodansha International. 1992.

Nitsch, Twylah. *Creature Teachers: A Guide to the Spirit Animals of the Native American Tradition.* Continuum Publishing Company. 1998.

Robertson, Olivia. *Sophia: Cosmic Consciousness of the Goddess.* CreateSpace Independent Publishing Platform. 2014.

Watkins, Alfred. *Early British Trackways, Moats, Mounds, Camps, and Sites.* Simpkin, Marshall, Hamilton, Kent & Co. 1922.

Wilson, Nigel, ed. *Encyclopedia of Ancient Greece.* Routledge. 2006.

Wolpert, Stanley, ed. *Encyclopedia of India.* Charles Scribner's Sons. 2006.

INDEX

Morita, Kiyoko, 114
Morrigan, 165
Mountain meditation, 58–59
Mountain priestess, 62
Music, 184–85

Na'ashjéii Asdzáá, 205
Nature
    connection to, 15–20, 37–43,
        52–53, 132–33, 153–54,
        205–6
    god of, 38, 44, 209
    as healer, 37–38
Nereus, 122
Night, 193
Nine Noble Virtues, 43–46
Nyx, 193

Oak faeries, 38, 44, 53
Oak trees, 52–53
Oceans, 119–29, 134
Ogham, 18
Oreades, 62
Orion, 183

Paganism
    age of, 191
    forms of, 43–44
    pagan deities, 53
    pagan lore, 38
    pagan prayer, 195
    pagan rites, 52, 191, 194, 197
    pagan sites, 53
    pagan symbolism, 31, 116
    pagan traditions, 103, 122

trees in, 38, 43–44, 52
virtues of, 43–46
Pan, 38, 44, 209
Pathways, 59, 114, 139–44
Pendulum, creating, 70–74
Pendulum psychometry, 72–74
Pentacle, 207–9
Pentagram, 40, 207–10, 221–22
Persephone, 15, 23, 29, 104,
    165
Phanes, 193
Phidias, 209
Planck, Max, 177
Planetary correspondences,
    185–86
Plants. *See also* Herbs
    cycle of, 15, 25, 44
    flowering plants, 79, 194–97
    healing properties of, 190–91
    magiferous plants, 190–91,
        200
    ritual for, 194–97
    verbenae, 194–97
Pleiades, 183
Pleione, 183
Pliny the Elder, 53, 189
Ponds, 121–23
Poseidon, 121
Power, cone of, 153–54
Priestesses
    bee priestess, 110–11
    of forest, 38
    high priestess, 153–54, 161
    of mountain, 62
    of sea, 122
Protection meditation, 100–103
Psyche, 28–29

scrying and, 127
spells for, 127–30, 134–35
for spiritual awakening,
123–25
for spiritual blessing, 127–30
swimming test, 127
Water witching, 128
Watkins, Alfred, 139–43
Western Herbal Medicine,
210–11. *See also* Herbal
medicine
Wheel of the Year, 99
Wiccan culture, 24, 100
Wiccan Rede, 43, 103, 205
Wiccan year, 15
Wind. *See also* Air
Four Winds, 86–90
god of, 84
invoking, 89–90
meditation and, 82–83
nymphs and, 87–88
power of, 82–83, 89–90, 95
realm of, 75–95
rituals for, 84–88
witches and, 75–95
Winds of Change, 89–90
Witches
brews of, 210–18
ethics of, 43–44
folk-lore and, 141, 153–54
as healers, 206, 210–18
herbs and, 75–95
moon and, 165–66, 172–73
sticks of, 44–46
transformation of, 150–51
wind and, 75–95
Woodland
apotropaic charm, 52–53

god of, 38–44, 105, 209
grounding ritual, 50–53
meditation in, 39–43
nymphs of, 38, 44, 53
oak trees, 52–53
realm of, 35–53
rituals for, 43–53
spells for, 48–49
tree augury, 43–47
Wynfrith, 53

Yemaya, 121

Zephyrus, 84
Zeus, 23–24, 99–100
Zodiac correspondences, 186
Zoomorphism, 103

ABOUT THE AUTHOR

Judy Ann Nock is the author of *The Modern Witchcraft Guide to the Wheel of the Year*, *The Provenance Press Guide to the Wiccan Year*, and *A Witch's Grimoire: Create Your Own Book of Shadows*. She has a bachelor's degree in theater and creative writing from Florida State University and is currently pursuing a master's degree from The City College of New York. Born in Philadelphia, Nock grew up in Pensacola, Florida. She lives in Manhattan.